CW00631524

BOB DWYER

THE
WINNING WAY

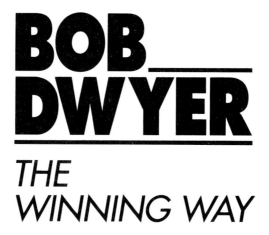

BOB DWYER

THE WINNING WAY

rugby press limited
Auckland

© 1992 Rugby Press Ltd and Bob Dwyer
First published in 1992 by Rugby Press Ltd
67-73 View Road, Glenfield, Auckland, New Zealand.

Layout/design and typesetting by Sportz Graphics Ltd,
Glenfield, Auckland.
Cover art by Grant Hanna, Auckland.
Printed by Australian Print Group, Victoria, Australia.

Rugby Press Ltd is a member of the Medialine Group of
companies. P.O. Box 100-243, North Shore Mail Centre,
Auckland 10, New Zealand.

ISBN 0-908630-41-7

To the Rugby family – past, present and future.

*To my own wife, Ruth, and my family, whose encouragement
and support in the past, in the present and, no doubt in the
future, has made everything possible.*

ACKNOWLEDGEMENTS

*The idea for this book came about as a result of the Wallabies'
success in the 1991 Rugby World Cup.
I guess, though, there has been a story there for some time now,
just waiting to be told.
There is no guessing, however, in my statement that without the
experience, literacy, encouragement and criticism of Phil Derriman
that the book would never have been written. Phil is a Sydney
journalist who writes regularly on cricket, but it was to Phil as a
Rugby enthusiast — and occasional writer and interested analyst —
that I turned for assistance and advice. This was eagerly accepted
and generously given, and I shall be ever grateful.
I must acknowledge, further, the dedicated assistance of my wife,
Ruth, in the reading of the first manuscript, and for her (often
hilarious) criticisms and advice for the many rewrites.*

CONTENTS

FOREWORD

A room. My boots. A telephone call.

"Of course, Bob, I would be honoured to write a foreword for your book. After these World XV games against the All Blacks I'll be going straight to Fiji for a family holiday so if you could get the manuscript to Angie I'll read the book while I'm over there."

It proved to be a big mistake.

There I was, assuming the classic holiday position of being stretched out under a palm tree while reaching for my third beer, when all of a sudden I was so overcome by guilt I had to put my ale down.

As you will soon discover in these pages, Bob is a stickler for preparation - "I don't want people who want to win, I want people who want to prepare to win" - and I was reminded all too vividly that bare months from tests against Scotland, New Zealand and South Africa, this probably wasn't what Bob had in mind.

When I got back from my run along the beach half an hour later, it was to find my wife teary-eyed. She had just finished the opening chapter of Bob's book which recalls some particularly emotional moments during the 1991 World Cup. Angie and our daughter Jessica had been with us in the United Kingdom and Ireland for some of that time and had gone through a lot of the highs and lows which Bob's written recollections had brought emotionally flooding back.

For readers not directly involved in the World Cup I am not sure this book will either make you go for a run or set you a-crying. But at the very least it should evoke in you some feeling of what it was like during that incredible time.

And not just the summit of Everest either. From base camp to the top Bob has lived through "interesting times" in Australian rugby, to say the least.

Since our return from the World Cup I have commented publicly about Dwyer's input during 1991 on many occasions. It seems to be rugby critics are always commentating on a player's 'form' and only very rarely on the form of a coach. Bob Dwyer has been my national coach since 1988 and in my opinion had by far his finest season in 1991. Some will say that it is an obvious observation to make after we had won the Cup, but for me, as with a winger by the name of Campese, without Dwyer's contribution, we may not have held aloft the Webb Ellis trophy on November 2, 1991.

We of Australian rugby are also indebted to Dwyer's foresight and judgement in advancing the representative careers of young players who became instrumental in our 1991 success. Players like Tim Horan, Jason Little, Willie O, Phil Kearns and Tony Daly were, if not in all cases "discovered" by Dwyer, at the very least put by him on a super highway straight into the test team ensuring that they were experienced and blooded when we needed them most.

For the first time, *Bob Dwyer - The Winning Way* is Bob's turn to get on the microphone and give his views on all the events and controversial occurrences in recent Australian rugby history. It provides a fascinating insight into the experiences of the former Randwick player and coach and the twice Australian national coach - his feelings and emotions at having 10 leading players withdraw at the 11th hour from a touring party in 1982, his "dismissal" in 1984 and "resurrection" in 1988 culminating in World Cup jubilation in 1991.

Despite the Wallabies' recent success it is reassuring that Dwyer is not carried away and, being a perfectionist, is far from satisfied with his team's World Cup performances. He is hell bent on correcting some of our technical inadequacies in the upcoming season. If by chance the 1992 Wallabies happen to get it right for 80 minutes under the guidance of Dwyer then I pity the opposition.

Happy reading

Nick Farr-Jones
Sydney, 1992

SWEET VICTORY

Once the cheering was over and the 1991 World Cup had begun to recede into history, it was obvious to all of us that the ultimate beneficiary of Australia's victory was Australian Rugby itself. I cannot think of a single sporting event that has had a bigger impact on a sport. Rugby's profile in Australia has risen to a height I would not have thought possible as recently as ten years before, when I first coached an Australian team. The parade through the centre of Sydney after our return demonstrated this. All of us who took part in it were overwhelmed. Players I spoke to afterwards told me that for the whole of the parade they were alternately laughing and crying and were powerless to prevent themselves doing either. While they were away playing in the World Cup they heard of the tremendous public support they were receiving back in Australia. Now they were experiencing it at first hand.

The players and I knew we had done something special. The pleasing thing about our victory was that other people thought we had done something special, too. As far as I know, every Rugby writer in the British press agreed that the World Cup had been won not merely by the best team on the day but by the best team in the tournament. I heard this view expressed dozens of times by Rugby people in Britain. You might argue about incidental matters such as whether or not the referee in the final should have awarded England a penalty try, but you could not argue whether or not the better side won.

Victory in an event as significant as the World Cup produces a strange flow of emotions. The players and I felt happy enough immediately afterwards. I know this if only because we look reasonably happy in photographs taken at the time. Yet my mood, and I think the mood of all the players, was strangely non-euphoric. The press men in the dressing room noticed this. 'You don't look to be feeling the way we think you ought to be feeling,' one of them said to me. One reason, I think, was that everyone in the Australian camp was a little disappointed at how we

The parade through Sydney after the World Cup triumph - all of us who took part in it were overwhelmed.
Col Whelan

played against England in the final. We won, but we should have won better. England had most of the ball, and we spent much of the second half holding out. After our outstanding performance against the All Blacks in the semi-final, we had hoped to finish off the tournament with something of a bang, and this did not happen.

Another reason, probably the main one, was psychological. If you have devoted years to pursuing a goal that is extraordinarily difficult to achieve, and if at last you achieve it, you find yourself thinking, 'Well, what comes next?' Mountaineers probably experience the same feeling when they climb to the top of a mountain and find there is nothing left to climb. I remember snapping out of this mood late the next day, when I was having a drink at the hotel bar with a few Australian supporters, one of whom, I remember, was Tim Horan's mother, Helen. Someone said: 'Well, nobody can argue about it now —we're definitely the champions of the world.' It was then that the real significance of our victory dawned on me. At that moment, for the first time, I felt truly elated.

The strain of the tournament took its toll. Nick Farr-Jones was one who suffered in this way. The pressure on him had been building up steadily during the tournament. The further we advanced towards the finals, the greater the attention which the media tended to focus on us. By the time we met England in the final I felt Nick was suffering from stress to the point where he was actually in physical decline. It was said he was suffering from a virus complaint, but I was not at all convinced that the cause of the complaint was a virus. On the evening of the World Cup final,

The magic moment. Nick Farr-Jones holds the Webb Ellis Trophy aloft after our defeat of England in the Twickenham final. Allsport

when we were driving in the team bus to an official dinner, he complained of feeling ill. Half an hour after the dinner began he turned to Michael Lynagh and said, 'I'm sick — I'm going to have to leave. You'll have to make the speech.' Faced suddenly with this responsibility, Michael implored him to stay, but Farr-Jones was too ill to remain. In the event, Lynagh took his place at the microphone and performed very well.

The impact which the World Cup telecasts made on the Australian public was amazing. I have felt the effect of it in a number of odd ways myself. Since returning from the World Cup I have repeatedly been stopped in the street by strangers wanting to talk Rugby. I have been asked for autographs in carparks and shopping centres. Once, when I stood up in my seat at a cricket match in Sydney, I was applauded by surrounding spectators. When someone who is not even a player receives this kind of attention, we may be sure that the public's awareness of the game has soared. This is true even in cities such as Melbourne where Rugby has only a tiny following. Some time after returning to Australia I was voted an associate membership of the Sport Australia Hall of Fame, and I went down to Melbourne to accept it. A young woman working there said to me, 'Before the World Cup I had never watched a Rugby match in my life. Now I'm determined never to miss watching a Rugby match whenever Australia is playing.' It seems there were many thousands of people in Melbourne just like her, people who were introduced to the game by the World Cup telecasts and took an immediate liking to it.

At a sports function that same evening a former Australian Football champion, Bob Skelton, presented an award. The person he presented it to was not a Rugby player, yet Skelton used the occasion to speak about Rugby. He said the World Cup telecasts had demonstrated once and for all that Australian Football was truly deprived in one important respect, and this was that the people who played the game could never take part in a genuine international tournament like the Rugby World Cup. If he had been a Rugby League identity, and if he had been honest, he would have to have said exactly the same thing.

Rugby League supporters followed the tournament avidly. I could not count the number of Rugby League people who came up to me and said that the tournament had opened their eyes to Rugby, that they had never realised what a great game it was. Yet the people who were most impressed, in my opinion, were Rugby people themselves. Clearly, it has recharged their enthusiasm for the game on a grand scale. Evidence of this has appeared in all sorts of ways. Just the other day I was told by a club official that many players who were about to retire had decided to keep going, albeit in one of the lower grades. These veterans had watched the Wallabies on television and felt inspired to go on. I wish them good luck and good fun.

The team which wins the next World Cup is going to have to do something special in its preparation. I say this in the firm belief that the kind of advances made between the first and second World Cups will be made again between the second and third. I thought the standard of preparation of the teams in 1991 was streets ahead of the preparation in 1987, and this was reflected in the standard of play. In 1987 the All Blacks were easily the best-prepared team, and they won decisively. In 1991 it was no coincidence that the two best-prepared teams, Australia and England, contested the final, and that the better prepared of these two teams won. I am not saying Australia in 1991 was definitely a better team than the All Blacks in 1987. They may have been or, as many New Zealanders would argue, they may not. It is a question open to debate. What I am sure about is that the general standard of play in the tournament was degrees higher than four years before. Canada played so much better than in 1987, for instance, and so did England.

After the New Zealanders won so impressively in 1987 the rest of the Rugby world set about trying to find out how they went about it — how they prepared their team. Since 1991, the rest of the Rugby world has been turning to us, seeking to discover our secrets. They began to do this even before the World Cup. When we beat Wales, England and then New Zealand so convincingly at home in 1991, there was a sudden upsurge of overseas interest in our preparation methods. One country, France, had taken a special interest in us two years earlier, in 1989, after our tour there. Back in Australia, there was a general feeling that Australia had performed poorly. In France, even while we were there, good judges of the game expressed the view that we would be favourite to win the World Cup in 1991. They must have known something.

After Australia won the World Cup, an English Rugby writer named Tony Bodley made the following observation: 'England lost the World Cup, valiantly, courageously at Twickenham last Saturday. The Wallabies won the World Cup a long, long time ago.' This struck a chord with me when I read it for it was entirely true. We did start winning the World Cup years before the team ever set off for the 1991 tournament. I hope that we will continue to win it for years afterwards — that Rugby in Australia will continue to reap the benefits of the victory. This is what makes the victory so sweet for all of us.

* * * *

Winning the World Cup in 1991 was almost certainly the greatest achievement by an Australian team in more than a hundred years of international Rugby. Some would also argue that the 1991 team was the strongest Australia has fielded. This isn't a matter anyone can be definite about, for there is simply no accurate means of comparing teams across the generations. I do believe, however, that it is possible to make some valid comparisons with one of the other great Australian teams of history, the 1984 side which won the grand slam in the British Isles, for that team is still fresh in the memory. It is an interesting comparison to make, for it helps to show us the direction Australian Rugby has been heading.

Which was the better side, Andrew Slack's 1984 Australians or Nick Farr-Jones' 1991 Australians? In assessing the record of each side, it is essential to first consider the relative strength of the opposition. Without doubt the standard of opposition faced by Australia in 1984 was generally poor. I have heard the view expressed that the England team that year was one of the weakest England sides of all time. On the other hand, you can only beat the team that the opposition puts on the field against you. Similarly, there is no point to be made from the fact that winning the World Cup was a greater achievement than winning the grand slam. In 1984, there was simply no World Cup for the Australian team to contest.

A good judge of the game can always assess quality in a team, regardless of the standard of the opposition, and the quality of the 1984 Wallabies was undoubtedly high. Mark Ella's performances on the tour were marvellous. Without him, Australia would have been a much lesser side. Our front row was extremely strong, Nick Farr-Jones and Steve Tuynman were effective at the back of the scrum, and Roger Gould played well at fullback.

Roger Gould . . . an outstanding contributor to the Wallabies' Grand Slam successes in the UK in 1984.   *Mike Brett*

As a general comment, I feel confident in saying that the 1991 team was bigger and stronger than the team of 1984, and I would like to think it played a more structured and more accurate type of game. I am also sure that the 1991 team was generally more athletic than the team of 1984. I do concede that improvements in preparation methods have had a lot do with this, so it is probably unfair to dwell on this point. Instead, it makes more sense to compare the teams in detail, position by position.

Everyone agrees that the 1984 front row was outstanding by world standards. The 1991 team had a very good front row also, and frankly I doubt whether there was much, if any, difference between them in scrummaging. I do think that the 1991 front row was more mobile than the front row of 1984. Topo Rodriguez might dispute this, for he was certainly a very mobile and skilful front rower who would have found a place in any team and, in fact, would have to be a candidate for an all-time world XV. It is fair to say, however, that Phil Kearns and Ewen McKenzie had more mobility and ball skills between them than Tommy Lawton and Andy McIntyre.

Of the second-rowers, John Eales would certainly have out-jumped

John Eales . . . would have out-jumped Steve Cutler in the lineouts. Photosport

Steve Cutler in the lineouts. The other second-rowers, Rod McCall and Steve Williams, would have been more or less evenly matched. McCall was probably a better lineout jumper than Williams, but Williams might well have had the upper hand in general play. In the back row, there was one player who played in both teams, Simon Poidevin, and I do not believe that Poidevin ever in his life played better than he did in 1991. When I look at the rest of the back row, I am inclined to the view that Tim Gavin and Willie Ofahengaue might have won a points decision over Steve Tuynman and David Codey. I know some people would contest this, yet it is fair to observe that Codey, fine player though he was, was not necessarily a world XV candidate whereas Ofahengaue seems to be in everyone's world XV. Gavin and Tuynman were both outstanding players whom I would find hard to separate.

Let us look now at the centres. I am prepared to argue that our centres at the World Cup, Tim Horan and Jason Little, were superior as a pair to Michael Lynagh and Andrew Slack in 1984. I say that partly because of their superiority in defence, which I do not think anyone would deny, and partly because of their superior speed. This is not in doubt — Horan and Little were clearly much faster than Lynagh and Slack. On the other hand, Lynagh even in 1984 was a more skilful player than Horan, although I do not think that would offset the other disadvantages.

I also haven't any doubt that the David Campese of 1991 was a better player than the David Campese of 1984 and that the Nick Farr-Jones of 1991 was a far better player than the Nick Farr-Jones of 1984. As Nick describes it himself, he ran on to the field in his first Test then thinking to himself, 'Oh my God, I'm going to make a fool of myself and embarrass my parents and my brothers and my university mates, and I should really be back at Wentworthville playing second division, and what on earth am I doing here anyway?' His fears were unfounded. He played very well in 1984, but he was still a vastly better player in 1991.

The 1984 team did have three great backs which any Australian team of any era would find hard to match — Mark Ella at five-eighth, Roger Gould at fullback and Brendan Moon at wing. (Moon was injured on the tour and had to fly home, but, for the purpose of this exercise, we shall include him in the 1984 team, just as I have included Gavin in the 1991 team, even though he was out of the World Cup side with an injury.) Allowing for the fact that Campese was a better player in 1991, I think the wingers in 1991, Campese and Rob Egerton, might have been roughly a match for Moon and Campese. Gould was outstanding, yet Marty Roebuck is reliable and highly effective. The difference between them would not be significant.

Which brings us to Ella and Lynagh. Many people might assume I would unhesitatingly prefer Ella. He was, after all, a player whose extraordinary skills were tailor-made for the type of game I try to coach. Yet

Michael Lynagh . . . possesses most of Mark Ella's running skills and is superior in kicking.   Mike Brett

Mark Ella, a player whose extraordinary skills were tailor-made for the type of game I try to coach.　　　　　　　　　　　　　　　　　Mike Brett

I find a choice between these two the toughest choice of all. Lynagh possesses all of Ella's handling skills, and while he may not possess all of Ella's running skills he does possess most of them and, moreover, he is clearly Ella's superior in kicking. I prefer to call the contest between these two a draw.

When all things are considered, I suppose there is not a great deal separating the two sides. The 1991 team was certainly fitter, for reasons I referred to before, and it may have just had an edge on the 1984 team in defence. If the two teams were to play each other, I suspect Lynagh and Slack in the centres might have had trouble coping in defence against the 1991 backline. Having said that, my mind at once goes back to the third Test against New Zealand in 1986, when a team more or less the same as the 1984 team defended as well as any Australian side I have seen.

In a three-Test series, I would expect the 1991 side to just beat the 1984 side, maybe by two Tests to one. It would be a privilege to coach either of them.

2

THE RANDWICK GAME

During the first part of our tour of Britain in 1988 the Wallabies did not play at all well. We lost the Test against England and moved on to play a Test in Scotland. Clearly, something decisive had to be done at this point to improve our game. We dropped a few players and shifted a few of the others around, and I laid down the law about the type of performance expected of everyone in the team. From then, we did not lose a match. Towards the end of the tour we attended a dinner in Cardiff after playing the Barbarians there, and I sat between between Tom Kiernan, a former captain and coach of Ireland who was president of the Irish Rugby Union, and George Morgan, immediate past president of the Welsh Rugby Union. During the dinner Tom Kiernan spoke to me about our backline play. 'We've never seen anything like it before,' he said. 'We've learnt a lot from visiting teams over the years, particularly the New Zealanders and South Africans, but it's always been about various elements of forward play and things like playing aggressively and being fit. No team has ever come and shown us a new type of backline play. Where does it come from?'

At this point George Morgan on the other side of me spoke up, saying, 'Tom, I've seen that type of backline play many times before.' Kiernan asked him where, and he explained he had been to Australia earlier that year and had visited the Randwick club in Sydney where he was given a copy of a video entitled *Randwick: The First Sixty-Five Years*. There were dozens of bits of film on the video, he said, which showed Randwick backlines playing precisely in this way. I told Morgan he was right. The type of backline play used by the 1988 Wallabies had certainly been used for many years by the Randwick team. But Randwick was not the first to use it. Its origins stretched at least as far back as the early 1920s, when it was used in Test matches by the All Blacks. In Rugby, as in most other fields of human endeavour, there was nothing new under the sun.

The features of our backline play which Tom Kiernan observed were, one, that the backs did not stand deep and, two, that they ran straight. There is much more to the concept than this, of course, but these are the most obvious characteristics of it. I have tried to trace the history of this style of play. As I said before, it was used by the All Blacks in the early 1920s and was picked up by the very successful Australian teams of the late 1920s and early 1930s. Later in the 1930s it was used by Randwick teams.

Subsequently, for whatever reason, this type of backline play was abandoned everywhere. It was certainly not used by Randwick teams in the 1960s when I was a player. The Randwick backline then used to stand deep. It is interesting to recall that Randwick in those days had a reputation for being vulnerable. Any team which played Randwick, no matter where it was placed in the Sydney competition, gave itself a reasonable chance of knocking Randwick over. Nobody thinks of Randwick as being vulnerable today.

The person who introduced me to the concept was a great player of the past named Cyril Towers, who had played centre for Randwick and for Australia in the 1930s when both teams were using this type of backline play. In his later years Towers often came down to the Randwick club to do a bit of coaching or simply yarn with the players about Rugby and how he thought the game should be played. No matter how many points we had won by, Cyril would always tell us we were no good. As a Randwick player in the 1960s I often found myself talking to him about technique and tactics, and it was during these conversations that he started telling me about the backline game he had played thirty years or more before. At first I regarded what he was saying as the ramblings of an old footballer, and as captain of the reserve-grade side I sometimes had quite heated arguments with him about it when he was assigned to coach us. On one of these occasions, I remember, Cyril stormed off saying that for as long as he lived he would never again coach a team in which Bob Dwyer was a player.

I was inquisitive enough, however, to continue speaking to him about his theories and turning them over in my mind. I must say that Cyril did not make this easy for me, because he was one of those teachers who preferred to tell his pupils what to do rather than explain to them why they should do it. The logic of what he was saying must have gradually seeped into my thinking, however, because one day, probably about 1975, I realised I had grasped it. Suddenly, it was obvious to me that Cyril's concept of backline play was right, and as soon as I accepted that fact it opened up a different world of analysis for me. At once there was a new scope for moving and manipulating opposition defences. The challenge was to get the opposition to react in the way you wanted them to react, as if they were puppets on a string. The extra dimension which this adds to the game gives enormous satisfaction to the players, because they feel they are doing something above the ordinary, so they have an incentive to try harder and play better.

*Cyril Towers, who introduced me to the concepts of backline play which I
have always applied as a coach.*   John Fairfax Group

I must make it clear that the principles I learned from Cyril Towers applied to one specific area of play — namely, open-side attack by the backline with the ball in hand. This is just a small part of the game as a whole, and it represents only a small part of my input as coach. Because the type of backline play I teach is the most conspicuously different element of my coaching, it is the one I have come to be identified with. Even so, many people have misunderstood it. Some have equated my backline play with running Rugby, but it actually has little in common with running Rugby as the term is generally understood. Most people, when they think of running Rugby, think of backs standing deep and running long distances. I advocate something quite different.

The essential features of my backline play, at least as seen by the spectator, are that the backs line up much flatter than is considered normal and that they then run straight. Lining up flatter means the backs have less distance to cover to get in front of the advantage line. It also means that they put the defence under pressure, because the defenders do not have time to draw a bead on them. There is much more to the concept than lining up flat and running straight, yet it is remarkable how quickly a backline can improve its performance just by doing this much.

There are two simple principles underlying the strategy. The first is that an attacking team cannot put the opposing defence under pressure until it comes under pressure itself. The second principle is that any attacking team has a natural advantage in numbers. It can always inject the fullback or the blind winger, or both, into the backline and so end up with an extra man, or men. The opposition cannot do this in defence, of course, because, not knowing where the attacking team is going to direct the ball, it has to keep all parts of the field covered. It has to have a fullback in the fullback's position and a blind-side winger. Once the attacking movement is under way, however, the attacking team begins to lose its advantage in numbers whenever an attacking player passes the ball without in some way engaging a defender. If there are five attacking players opposed by four defenders and the first attacking player passes the ball without occupying the first defender, then clearly there are only four attacking players left, who are still opposed by four defenders. If the second attacking also passes the ball without engaging a defender, the attacking players will then be outnumbered by the defenders by four to three. Unless a defender misses a tackle, the chances of an attacker getting through are small.

In a Test against New Zealand at Concord Oval in 1988, Gary Ella received the ball and was tackled by no fewer than four All Blacks — Michael Jones, Grant Fox, John Schuster and Joe Stanley. In other words, our outside-centre was tackled by their flanker, five-eighth, inside-centre and outside-centre. Somebody said to me later that he did not think Gary Ella had much of a game. It is not easy to have a good game, I replied, when

John Kirwan . . . we'd snap him up if he wasn't wanted by the All Black selectors.
                                                                        Peter Bush

there are four defenders on your shoulder. The problem was simply that our five-eighth and inside-centre had not threatened the defence at all.

John Kirwan had to contend with exactly the same problem in the semi-final of the 1991 World Cup, and afterwards I heard some commentator say he had not played well. I thought Kirwan played wonderfully well. I could not count the number of times he broke through the first two tackles, but there were always two other Australian defenders on top of him. Surely you cannot expect anyone to beat four tackles. I believe Kirwan went into print later saying that unless John Hart was made coach he would not play for New Zealand again. I wondered when I read this what chance we might have of talking him into emigrating to Australia. If he did not want to play for New Zealand, we would certainly give him a game. He is a fine player.

I have yet to speak to anyone able to refute the logic of the concept. Some argue that this type of play is fraught with danger because it has to be performed under pressure. My response is that there are degrees of pressure. If I pass the ball to a team-mate when there is a defender right on top of him and about to barrel him, then, sure, he's under pressure. But if I pass the ball to him when the defender is still two metres away, which means he has time to catch the ball and change the angle of his run to avoid the tackle, is he then under pressure? I do not believe so. The critics then say, 'But he might get tackled and drop the ball.' I answer that, one, we can teach him not to drop the ball and that, two, we positively want him to be tackled. A soccer player once said to me, 'When are Rugby players going to realise that attackers should run at defenders, not away from them?' I answered, 'I haven't any idea, but if you ever find out please let me know, because I've been trying to get them to realise that for years.'

Soccer players understand that attackers need to run *at* defenders. Conversely, defenders in soccer spend most of their time on the field trying to get out of the way of attackers. The biggest mistake they can make is to be drawn into an attacker, which is why you so often see defenders in soccer running backwards. In Rugby, typically, an attacker will run to avoid a defender. As a result, he draws the defender not only to himself but to the team-mate running alongside him to whom he is about to pass the ball.

In 1981, while watching the Wallabies' tour of Britain on television, I saw the worst example of this I can remember. The match was between Ireland and Australia, and Simon Poidevin was playing flanker. From the back of the lineout, Poidevin was able to cover, in turn, Ireland's five-eighth, inside-centre, outside-centre and fullback, without another Australian defender even coming into the picture. The net result for Ireland was that Australia ended up with four extra defenders, namely the opposite numbers of all these Irish players who had not been drawn in. This left the Irish winger in a fearful predicament, for he not only had this wild, red-headed flanker charging down on him but four or five other defenders as well. Once, when one of the Irish wingers was about to be set up in this way, I saw him run ahead of the ball, and I wondered at the time if he did it deliberately, realising what was in store for him. This made no difference to the fullback, however. He passed the ball anyway, even though the winger was about two metres in front of him.

The next Test the Wallabies played on that tour was against Wales. The Welsh five-eighth stood as deep as the Irish five-eighth had done, but he carried the ball a long way and, unlike his Irish counterpart, he straightened his run towards Poidevin before passing to the inside-centre. Poidevein was drawn to him each time, and as a result he made little impact in defence for most of that match. The contrast with what happened in the previous Test was, I thought, so striking that it provided a text-book illustration of how essential it is for backs to draw their opposing defenders.

In later years, I had many long discussions with Cyril about Rugby strategy. Some were at his home in Maroubra, where Cyril liked to demonstrate backline moves with coins on the top of the dining table. A salt shaker would represent the scrum, and the coins would be lined up in two opposing backline formations. Cyril then moved the coins about, showing me the angles at which the backs needed to run to produce the desired effect. He was very precise about angles and other details of each move. He would say that this winger needed to stay tight and not drift wide, because this would ensure the fullback was brought into the particular space he needed to attack through, and so on, and all the while he would be shifting the coins about on the table to illustrate the point he was making. Cyril Towers was an extremely single-minded man who had an exceptional grasp of the intricacies of the game. The legacy he has left to Australian Rugby is invaluable. We must not lose it.

3

THE COACHING BUG

I grew up against a background of Rugby League, not Rugby Union. My father, Ted, played first-grade League in Sydney for Canterbury-Bankstown. He was born in the bush, but came with his family to Sydney as a boy after his father died. I have no memories of my father as a player, but I do remember him coaching League teams in later years, mainly junior teams, in the Waverley area where I grew up. His most famous pupil was Ken McCaffery, the great League back of the 1950s. I remember approaching McCaffery for his autograph when he was only seventeen or eighteen years old, probably because my father had spoken to me of his tremendous potential. My older brother thought I was silly. 'You're not supposed to get autographs of blokes like that,' he said. 'You're supposed to get the autographs of the superstars.' I had watched young McCaffery play, however, and even then I thought of him as a star, if not yet a superstar.

Curiously, I have a very clear recollection of my father insisting as a matter of policy that all backline players should run straight. It is actually the only point of technique I can remember him making. No doubt he hammered it into his own players. Perhaps it made an impression on me, too. I may add here, to round off the story, that my father long ago became a convert to Rugby Union and, in particular, to Randwick Rugby. For years now he has rarely missed a senior match.

I had one of my first experiences of international Rugby Union when I went to the Sydney Cricket Ground to see the Springboks play Australia in 1956. They were playing under the so-called international law, which allowed players to kick out on the full, and I found the incessant kicking boring. As a spectacle, the match was appalling. The only Australian player I saw that day who seemed capable of holding his own with the opposition was Dick Tooth. In the following year Tooth was omitted from the Wallabies' tour of Britain and France, a decision which astonished me and which apparently disillusioned Tooth himself, for he never played

Rugby again in Australia. He was, in my view, a great loss to Australia. Unfortunately, no matter how well intentioned and well informed selectors may be, they are always liable to make absurd decisions — a fact which, since becoming a national selector myself, I have tried to keep in mind.

By this time I was in my mid-teens and was playing Rugby at school. My favourite sport, however, was cricket. As a boy I had always been better at cricket than at Rugby. I was just fifteen, for instance, when I made the first XI as a batsman-wicketkeeper at Waverley College, a Christian Brothers school in Sydney with a fine sporting tradition. Waverley College has produced not only top Rugby players (Cyril Towers was one of them), but top cricketers (Jack Fingleton, for instance, was a Waverley boy) and even a champion boxer, Tony Madigan, who went close to beating Cassius Clay at the 1960 Olympics. Yet Rugby was certainly the school's lifeblood. Every boy was compelled to play it unless he was able to produce a doctor's certificate declaring he was unfit to do so. Even this was not enough in many cases. Boys who produced doctors' certificates were usually urged to obtain a second opinion. This kind of compulsion might seem unacceptable to many people today, but it did have some positive effects. It produced a great feeling of unity within the school, for instance, because boys were not thought any the worse for playing in the Fs or the Gs. We took as much pride in the Fs if they played well as we did in the As. I am pleased to say this same tradition exists at Randwick. We can feel as delighted when the fifth-graders have a great game as when the first-graders do.

At Waverley, I developed a love of Rugby, but I did not manage to advance beyond the fourth XV. In my final year at school, in 1957, I transferred to Sydney High, and there I made the first XV. Like many schoolboys, I did not really find my feet in Rugby until I started to grow, an event which, in my case, took place with surprising speed in the summer of 1956-57. Thereafter, I became increasingly interested in the game. In 1959, after leaving school, I began playing for the Randwick colts, or juniors as they were known then — a step I took not because of any special affinity with Randwick but simply because some of my friends had gone to Randwick to play. It was, as things turned out, a fateful step. I went on to play for Randwick for eighteen years, nearly always as a flanker. In all, I turned out for Randwick in 347 senior matches.

For most of the time I played for Randwick it never occurred to me that I would ever coach a team. I was involved in Rugby purely because I enjoyed playing. I can say honestly that I did not have any ambitions to play representative Rugby. In fact, I have a clear memory of being astonished when I was told during the 1964 season that I had been promoted to the first-grade side. From the outset, I was attracted by the intellectual challenge which Rugby presented as a tactical game. I was keen enough in 1959, I recall, to go along to watch the touring British

Helping out in the position I knew best, flanker. It's where I packed down
for Randwick for 18 years. Robert Pearce, John Fairfax Group

Lions train. While I was in Ireland for the World Cup in 1991 I was
delighted to meet several veterans of that Lions tour. The 1959 Lions team
made a deep impression on me. I have a sharp recollection of sitting on the
Paddington Hill at the Sydney Cricket Ground with a few mates from the
Randwick Colts and watching Ken Catchpole, who had been playing with
us until the year before, play his first representative game as halfback for
New South Wales against the Lions. New South Wales won that day, and
Catchpole had a marvellous match. He scored one try and set up another
which was scored by Alan Morton. I can still name most of that Lions team
in their positions and, in fact, I did so when I met a few of them in 1991.
They seemed surprised that memories like this could last more than thirty
years.

In the mid-1970s the Australian Rugby Union started running a
coaching course and wrote to all the clubs inviting each of them to send
three people to attend. The Randwick club turned the invitation down,
believing its coaches would learn nothing from the course which they did
not already know. On hearing this, three Randwick players, including
myself, volunteered to go as Randwick's representatives, and the club
agreed. In fact, it proved to be an excellent course. I went back to

Randwick saying to the coaches there, 'You fellas missed the point. The course wasn't meant to tell you *what* to teach but merely *how* to teach it.' I have no doubt that it was while attending that course that I was bitten by the coaching bug.

Armed with the information I had acquired doing that coaching course, I pointed out to my team-mates at Randwick on my return that we were not scrummaging the right way — that we should be doing it another way. One of the team said, 'Look, Bob, we're simply not capable of scrummaging the way you suggest. Maybe the Australian team can do it, but they're the Australian team. We're just Randwick seconds.' I replied, 'Yes, but we're only playing Eastwood seconds. Surely it's as easy for us to scrummage the right way against Eastwood seconds as it is for the Australian team to scrummage correctly against the All Blacks. If it's right, it's right.' The player saw my point. I think that discussion may have amounted to my first venture into coaching.

In 1976 I turned out again for Randwick as a player. I was thirty-five then and, I suppose, regarded as one of the elders of the club. I was a committee member as well as the club's social secretary. Although I had graduated from University of NSW as an electrical engineer, I had decided to try to make a career in the real estate business, which meant my weekends would no longer be so free for playing Rugby. My playing days, I knew, were coming to an end. At the end of the 1976 season, Randwick's first-grade coach, Bob Outterside, decided to step down. As someone with a deep interest in the club's affairs, I and a few other senior players cast about for a new coach. I approached Peter Johnson, Ken Catchpole and Terry Reid, but none of these was interested. At this point I resolved that, if none of these well-credentialled people were going to stand, I would stand myself. I did, and won an exhaustive ballot against, I think, about eight other candidates. Thus, I became Randwick's first-grade coach in 1977 without ever having coached a Rugby team before. My only coaching experience of any kind was coaching a school Rugby League team, Marcellin College, for about four matches the year before.

When I started as coach in 1977, a Randwick official, Ron Meagher, spoke to me about the team's chances. He said he realised we had a team of relative unknowns and that we were in a stage of rebuilding but he wondered, rather tentatively, if we might have an outside chance of making the semi-finals. I answered that I was aiming much higher than that — that I felt we had a good chance of winning the grand final. I told him I guaranteed we would make the semi-finals. As things turned out, we did struggle, but we made it to the semi-finals and then to the grand final against Parramatta, who only just managed to beat us. We were only a few points behind and were pressing the Parramatta line towards the end of the match when one of their players intercepted a pass and scored, putting the match beyond reach.

I was still feeling my way to some extent in that first year, but I was able to introduce many of my own ideas. The first change I made was to get the team practising skills in the pre-season training. Previously, pre-season training had consisted almost entirely of fitness training. The players did not even touch a football. It was as if they were training to be athletes, not Rugby players. The skills training I introduced was hard work, and the players did get fit doing it, but they had also had fun. In this pre-season training we started developing tactics and strategies, which is something players always find enjoyable and motivating.

By the end of the season, I had the team playing the game more or less as I wanted it played. Even then Randwick had a great tradition of running the ball. If fact, Randwick ran the ball more then than it does now. I find it ironic that, although I am internationally recognised as a proponent of running Rugby, there are within my own club a number of stalwarts who accuse me of having abandoned the old Randwick running game. Of course, any team can run the ball. The important thing, as England discovered to its cost in the World Cup final in 1991, is how you run it.

In 1978, my second year, three brothers named Ella joined the club. It was the start of something big for all of us.

The Ella fellas - Gary, Glen and Mark. When they joined the Randwick club in 1978, it was the start of something big. John Fairfax Group

4

THE ELLAS

In 1977 word reached us at the Randwick club that a small state high school in our area, Matraville High, had an exceptionally talented Rugby XV. I remember Cyril Towers talking to me about the team one day and suggesting it might be worth looking over in case it contained one or two potential Randwick recruits. I therefore made a point of going to Randwick's training ground, Latham Park, one Wednesday afternoon when I heard that the Matraville High team was to play St Joseph's College, one of Sydney's most distinguished Catholic boys schools. However talented the Matraville boys might be, I knew St Joseph's would test their mettle. St Joseph's had, and still has, a fearsome reputation in Australian schoolboy Rugby for being tough, skilled, committed and invariably successful. Even if the Matraville boys were as good as I had been told, they would have to work hard to prove it.

When I arrived the match was already under way. The first thing that struck me was the difference in appearance of the two teams. The St Joseph's boys were fine young physical specimens — clean-cut, well-muscled and generally well turned-out. The Matraville team was, by comparison, a sorry sight.— a mob of skinny, little ragamuffins. There were, I also noticed, eight or nine Aboriginal boys among them. With the exception of one red-haired winger, all the backs were Aboriginal. I heard later that Matraville did not have a backline but a 'blackline with a red tip.'

Then I began observing the play. It was worth travelling far to see. The Matraville boys were not merely having the better of the contest. They were running rings around their opponents. For once, a St Joseph's first XV looked entirely bewildered. No matter what they did, they could not stop tries being scored. The scruffy Matraville High boys outclassed their opponents quite brilliantly and, moreover, they did it with ease. I came away impressed.

I would have been more impressed if I had known then that as many as nine of these Matraville boys would go on to play first-grade Rugby in

Sydney and that four would play for Australia. Given the fact that Matraville High had only fifteen boys in the final year in 1977, I cannot believe there has ever been a greater concentration of Rugby talent in one school. They were expertly coached by Geoff Mould, who had learnt much of his Rugby from Cyril Towers. Five of the Matraville boys were chosen in the now-famous Australian Schoolboys team which toured Britain later that year. Lloyd Walker, who went on to play for Australia, was not one of the five. Instead, the selectors chose a Queensland schoolboy named Wally Lewis. Long after Lewis became the biggest name in Australian Rugby League, he wrote how fortunate he was that Walker went to Matraville High. Lewis reasoned that the selectors, having chosen five boys from one school, were reluctant to choose a sixth. Walker would have been chosen ahead of him, he thought, if he had gone to any school but Matraville High.

I suppose I was aware that day that three of the Aboriginal boys playing for Matraville High were brothers, although I do not specifically recall it now. Before long I came to hear a lot about these brothers. Their name was Ella and they were, everyone said, unusually talented. The three Ellas were chosen to tour Britain with the Australian Schoolboys team in 1977, and it was obvious Randwick would be wise to enlist their services. During the 1977-78 off-season, having made an appointment with the boys' mother, May Ella, Gary Pearse and I drove down to see them at their home at La Perouse. We knew when we arrived that we had found the right house. There were about ten pairs of football boots on the front verandah.

It was taken for granted the brothers would join Randwick. What we needed to discuss with them was whether they would play grade or colts. We talked to two of the brothers in the living room. The third brother — I think it was Glen — stayed in a bedroom reading a book. I remember one of the brothers saying something like, 'I couldn't give a damn whether I played colts or grade,' whereupon Mrs Ella called out from some other part of the house, 'Don't you use that language in this home, thank you!' At once, I knew we were dealing with my kind of people. I told the two boys in the living room that they would be wasting their time playing colts. They would be so much better than the others, I said, that their talent wouldn't be extended and they would risk developing wrong technique. The two brothers agreed, and one of them called out to the third brother (we will assume it was Glen) in the bedroom: 'Hey, Glen. We're playing grade.' A voice in the bedroom answered back, 'Okay.' And so it was settled.

The Ella brothers duly presented themselves at Randwick before the 1978 season. They began by playing together in a club trial, which I watched sitting on the hill at Latham Park beside a club selector, John Cole, the former Australian winger. After a half-hour or so, I turned to Cole and said, 'These three Ella boys have got something unusual going here. I've been watching them, and they haven't stopped running since the game started. They don't seem to get tired.' It was true. The opposition would kick off, Glen at fullback would catch the ball, Mark and Gary would run back, Glen would pass it to Mark, he'd pass it to Gary, maybe one or two others in the team would get involved, the Ellas would back up, Mark would be passing it to Gary again, or Gary back to Mark, and suddenly they were over the line for a try. Then they'd run back into position to wait for the kick-off, and the exercise would be repeated. They never seemed to run above three-quarter pace, and at this pace they seemed capable of running forever.

We put them all into second grade to begin with. During the final trial match, however, one of Randwick's first-grade centres, John Hoare, dislocated his elbow, and Gary Ella took his place. Thus the youngest of the Ella brothers, Gary, who was about a year younger than the twins Mark and Glen, became the first of them to play first-grade. Gary was a rather scrawny youth then, just seventeen years old, but he performed exceptionally well. Within a month or two, he was joined in the first-grade side by his two brothers. In their first match together, Randwick thrashed Northern Suburbs by 63 points to nil. It was an amazing game. Northern Suburbs went into it unbeaten, and Randwick had been beaten only once, so the press saw it as possibly being a preview of the grand final. Almost every time Norths kicked the ball to Glen Ella at fullback, Randwick scored a try. After the full-time bell, Norths kicked again to Glen, and Randwick scored one more. It was a kind of football never witnessed in Sydney before — a close-quarter game of gentle passing, easy running and consistent support. The Ellas just kept running and passing and scoring, as they did in the Randwick trial.

The wonderful achievements of the Ella brothers are well documented, and there is no need for me to recount them here. They were profoundly gifted players who had acquired Rugby skills commensurate with their God-given talent. Mark was the most successful of them, of course. Gary played six Tests for Australia, but his career was, I think, permanently affected by the knee reconstruction he underwent at the age of seventeen. Glen had another kind of problem. His promotion to the Australian side was blocked by another player of outstanding ability, Roger Gould, who was already occupying the fullback position. Moreover, Glen was not so confident or determined a player as Mark.

What was their secret? They were, of course, uncannily talented. They were also extremely mature players, even as boys of seventeen or eighteen. I hold the view that experience is not necessarily a function of age, and when I tell people this I invariably cite the case of the Ellas to illustrate my point. As a general rule, the more often a player experiences pressure, the better he is able to cope with it, yet some players, like the Ellas, are already experienced as teenagers in the sense of being able to concentrate and

Gary Ella . . . a gifted player who was probably affected by having his knee reconstructed when he was 17.

remain composed under pressure. Others are unable to do this at thirty.

All three of them were really tough individuals. They looked so scrawny that opponents felt they could knock them about, but somehow they bounced back from all the heavy blows, as if they were made of Indian rubber. I think Glen was the toughest of the three. I also think that in some ways Glen was the most naturally gifted. During the Ellas' first year at Randwick, Glen was doing a tertiary course which prevented him arriving at training until quite late. I can see him clearly in my memory now, running up from the bus stop in Anzac Parade on Thursday evening with a knapsack containing his football gear slung over his back, leaping the fence and shouting to us as he ran to the changing rooms, 'I'll be back in a sec.' Like his brothers, he had an entirely pragmatic approach to the game. Once, when we were thinking of lining up the Randwick backline even closer to the defence, I asked Gary Ella whether he would still have time to get the ball through his hands. It is the player in his outside-centre position who is under greatest pressure in a flat backline alignment, because the ball is liable to reach him about the same time as the defence. Before Gary had time to answer, Glen spoke up: 'Well, if he can't manage it, he shouldn't be playing in that position.' For Glen, it was as straightforward as that.

The three brothers argued with each other constantly at training, but I know they had great respect for each other's ability. If Mark called for the ball from Glen, or if Gary called for the ball from Mark, he would be sure to get it.

In my view, Glen was the most talented runner of the three brothers. He possessed a beautiful balance which enabled him to step effortlessly off either foot. To see him running among opposition players, stepping off his left foot and his right foot in turn, was to be reminded of an ice skater. He did one thing on a Rugby field I have not seen performed by anyone else. If the opposition put up a high ball, he did not stand where the ball was going to land but perhaps four or five metres away. Then, at the last moment, he would swoop in and catch it. It must have been a most difficult manoeuvre, demanding perfect timing, but I often saw him evade opposing players charging the kick down in this way. I don't think Glen ever appreciated his own talent. He never realised how gifted he was. When he was chosen for the first time to play for Australia, he said to me, 'Why did you pick me? Why didn't you pick Roger?' I replied, 'Mate, we picked you because we think you're the best.'

Gary Ella was different. I used to think of him as a Rugby maestro. He understood his role at outside-centre perfectly and he under-played it with the aplomb of a classical pianist. I once drove a couple of players to a match, and on the way one of them, a reserve half-back, said, 'I don't think Gary's all that great a player. He doesn't seem to stand out.' I was interested in the comment, so I asked the other player, a winger, what he thought. He replied, 'Gary's a dream.' When you played outside Gary, the winger said, all you had to worry about was your opposite number. When you went to accelerate into the gap, the ball would be there, right in front of you. The winger summed up Gary accurately. If I were to write a textbook on positional play at outside-centre, I would use Gary Ella as the subject. He was not as fast as you would ideally want an outside-centre to be, although that could have been a legacy of his damaged knee. The outside of his knee was so badly torn that the doctors were able to fold up his lower leg so that the inside of his heel was touching his lower abdomen. It was a shocking injury for a seventeen-year-old.

Mark Ella, as we know, was in a class of his own. Mark was very correct in his play and very confident. He was also extremely coachable. You would have to correct him constantly, as you do every player, but unlike most players he always grasped at once what you were saying. You might

Glen Ella . . . probably the most talented of the three brothers.   Mike Brett

say to him, 'Mark, you're starting to run a bit early from the second-phase play," and he'd grumble, 'Okay, okay — I'll fix it.' He did fix it, because he understood the problem instantly. Another of his virtues was that he was terribly demanding of himself and his team-mates. In my opinion, this is an area where both coaches and players regularly fall down — they are not as demanding of excellence as they should be; they are prepared to accept second-best as best. As a twenty-year-old captain of Randwick, Mark Ella was fiercely demanding. At training, if one of his players got an angle slightly wrong or was half a metre out of position, Mark would call, 'Do it again! How many times do I have to tell you? This is what you're supposed to be doing.' Only the best would do.

Mark Ella was, like Glen, a beautifully balanced runner, and he had a superb change of pace. He was also blessed with a lovely running style. When he accelerated, he had a way of sinking his hips in a manner reminiscent of one of those prestige cars, which lower their suspension as they are about to take off. He also had a way of extending his legs out in front of him when he ran which, strangely enough, used to remind me of an emu. When he accelerated, he did not lean forwards and push off, as many runners do, but rather reached forwards with his legs in long, smooth strides. When New South Wales played Scotland at the Sydney Cricket Ground in 1982, Mark made a break against the run of play — it may have been with an intercept, I cannot now remember — and he set off for the try-line, which was about eighty metres away. He was chased by the Scottish winger Roger Baird, who at that time was one of the fastest runners in international Rugby. Baird could not catch him. Ella kept slowing down and speeding up, forcing Baird each time to change the angle of his run. As I recall, Baird was only about three paces from him for the last forty metres, yet somehow he could not get any closer. It was thrilling to watch.

One of Mark's greatest strengths as a player — and this was true of his brothers, too — was an intense power of concentration. It sometimes seemed to me that the Ellas had eyes like laser beams. If there was a loose ball, they would fasten their eyes on it, not allowing anything to distract them, and then pounce on it like birds of prey. This was also the reason they were such good ball handlers. If there was a ball bouncing around, it did not matter if they were shoved or jumped on or had their jerseys pulled, their concentration remained focused on the ball.

Mark played with a natural flair, but I think Rugby commentators have generally over-stated this dimension of his play. He was certainly not, as he has sometimes been depicted, a player to whom everything came so easily and naturally that he scarcely had to think what he was doing. His brilliance was by no means mindless brilliance. It was practised brilliance. About 1979, I arranged for a number of players and former players, all experts in their positions, to speak to the players occupying those positions

*Mark Ella . . . one of the most accomplished Australian rugby players I have
seen.* Mike Brett

Ella magic, at Japan's expense. Mark passes to Glen at the Hong Kong
sevens, and another try unfolds.   Peter Bush

in the various Randwick teams. Thus, someone with expertise in the
fullback position spoke to all the Randwick fullbacks, and so on. I had
trouble finding a former five-eighth who was available to come, so I asked
Mark Ella, a relatively new first-grade five-eighth, to do the job himself.
I made sure I was within earshot when Mark gave his lecture. He was only
nineteen years old, yet he spoke with precision about how he played the
position himself. He described things such as his angle of support, the
timing of the pass, the angle of his run, and so on, in detail. This was a
skilled operator talking, not some kind of free-spirited genius.

Ella was still a marvellous player when he made his comeback at
Randwick in the late 1980s. The last time he touched the ball for
Randwick he scored under the posts. He picked up a loose ball in a counter
attack, threw it to someone, looped around and took the ball again, sent
it out along the backline and finally backed up to take an inside pass from
the winger and go over the line. You could not have written a better script
for his farewell, for this was vintage Ella. It was as if he was giving us one
last reminder of just how wonderful a player he was.

Was Mark Ella the most accomplished Australian player I have seen?
I am not avoiding the question by saying that I could not separate him from
three or four others. Russell Fairfax is one of the others, and so is David
Campese. I would rate Campese first for pure individual brilliance, Ella for
mastery of the game's structure, Ken Catchpole for his all-round ability
and Michael Lynagh for his range of point-scoring skills, yet I find it
impossible to rate any of these above or below the others. Mark Ella would
have been proud to score the try which Lynagh scored in the final minutes
of the Ireland match in the 1991 World Cup. It was a classic Mark Ella-
type try. Lynagh did exactly what Ella would have done. I felt proud at the
time that there was a bit of Mark Ella in our World Cup victory.

5

THE POSITIVE APPROACH

R ugby is a game which deserves to be played positively, by which I
mean that every team should be willing to risk defeat in the pursuit
of victory. If your primary aim is to avoid defeat by avoiding risks,
you would be better off not playing Rugby at all. To set out to win by
capitalising on the mistakes of your opponents is, in my opinion, a
miserable way to play the game. I have a low opinion of Rugby teams whose
standard policy is: 'Let's boot the ball up to the other end of the field and
see if the other team makes a mistake, because even if they don't make a
mistake we won't really have lost anything.' My policy is: 'Let's play a
positive, aggressive game and let's create our own opportunities for
winning — let's keep the winning of the match in our hands.'

I have been critical of England in this respect. England's approach in
the 1991 World Cup was certainly aggressive, but the team relied heavily
on the other team making mistakes. They kept kicking the ball over the
top of the scrum, for instance, in the hope that an opponent would knock
on or be caught in possession, or commit some other error. I have a
contempt for this type of play. For one thing, it is simply too easy. Surely
there must be a more challenging way to win a match than kicking the ball
over the top of the scrum. My main objection to it, though, is the one that
I have previously explained — that it places the destiny of the match in
the other team's hands. By employing this kind of tactic, the England team
was effectively saying to its opponents: 'Whether we win or lose this match
doesn't depend on what we do with the ball but on what you do with it.'
It is an entirely negative approach to the game, and I find it disappointing,
for it neglects the opportunities the game has to offer. When I watched
England play in the World Cup I often had the impression that scoring was
not their primary objective. Against Scotland, they barely scored enough
points to win, and if Gavin Hastings had not missed a simple kick England
might not have made the final. It was only when it made the final against
Australia that I thought England really set out to score.

The time for a team to play positive and aggressive Rugby is not when it is trailing badly late in the second half but at the very start of the match when the score is nil-all. Watch closely the next time you see a player make a mistake, such as dropping the ball or missing a tackle, which enables the opposition to score. From the moment play restarts, you will invariably see this player outdo himself in an attempt to make up for the previous error. Typically, he will perform a ferocious tackle on the opposition player who catches the ball from the kick-off. The question this raises is: why did he wait until he committed an error before making such a great tackle? Instead of saying, 'I've done something wrong so I've got to atone for it,' he should have been saying, 'I've got to do something right and maybe we'll score.'

The success of the Wallabies in 1991 had a special significance for me personally, for it was an endorsement of the philosophy I had begun promoting in senior Rugby fifteen years before. At that time, and for some years afterwards, virtually everybody at the national level of the game in Australia seemed convinced that the method of play we were using at Randwick could never succeed in representative Rugby. The fact that Randwick had begun winning a string of Sydney premierships did not impress them. They simply dismissed it by saying: 'Well, maybe it works at the club level, but there's no way it can work at a higher level — and certainly not at the international level.' At the same time, there were others saying that it could not work at a lower level. They reasoned that my method demanded a degree of skill which teams below the first-grade club level did not possess.

I found it frustrating to have my ideas rejected out of hand by the conservative people influencing the game in Australia, simply because they did not understand them. I felt exasperated that other people were blind to things that were obvious to me. Many times I have sat in the Members Stand at the Sydney Cricket Ground and heard spectators around me applaud a player when he kicked the ball down the line and gained thirty metres. The fact he had an overlap when he kicked seemed to escape their notice altogether. Instead of possibly scoring a try, the team now had to contest a lineout with an opposition throw-in — and the spectators applauded the player responsible! Why? Because they were applauding something that was obvious to them. The opportunity for a try which went begging was not obvious to them.

My attitude is that a player should never be congratulated for a bad move, even if the move somehow results in a try. To do so is as illogical as applauding a batsman who scores a boundary with a bad stroke. I once captained Randwick in a match in which we scored a try from the back of the lineout. The player who set up the try had carried the ball around the back of the lineout in a way which was in total conflict with the way we had practised the move. For the next two minutes, while we walked back to our half and waited for the conversion attempt, I berated this player. 'Why bother coming to training?' I asked him. 'What's the point? We've practised this move a hundred times, and you decide to do a stupid thing which completely defeats the purpose of what we were trying to do.' The player was shocked. I think he had expected me to pat him on the back.

Looking back on it now, I suppose there could not have been a worse time than the late 1970s in which to introduce a concept of play as radical as the one I was advocating. At that time most influential people in Australian Rugby had an ultra conservative approach to the game. They regarded flair as being synonymous with vulnerability. They would not pick Mark Ella to play for Australia because they considered him vulnerable, so they picked Tony Melrose instead. This kind of thinking prevailed at the state level, too. At that time Mark Ella was playing five-eighth for New South Wales and Melrose inside-centre. Whenever New South Wales was defending its line, Melrose was brought into five-eighth and Ella would go to inside-centre. The fear was that Ella would take the wrong option. Because he was tremendously talented, it was automatically assumed he was tactically fragile.

Mercifully, this kind of thinking is not nearly so common today, but it has not disappeared completely. David Campese has continued to be a victim of it from time to time. One reason is that the highs of the very good players like Campese are much higher than everyone else's, which makes their lows seem very low by comparison. Willie Ofahengaue has been unfairly criticised for this very reason. People see him at his explosive, devastating best and somehow think that is the way he ought to be playing all the time. When he is not explosive and devastating, they think he is taking things easy. But this is not true. Watch Ofahengaue closely on the field and you will see he has a very high work rate. It is interesting how many action photos he appears in. If you examine photos taken of the Australians in their World Cup matches in 1991, you find that Ofahengaue appears in three-quarters of them, which is an indication to me of a player who is constantly part of the action.

Even my own Randwick players doubted at first whether playing the Dwyer game was feasible at the international level. Mark Ella was one of these. When he toured Britain for the first time with the Wallabies in 1981 I watched him play on television and noticed how deep he was standing. I phoned him one night at his hotel there and said, 'Mate, I've been watching the games on television. How come you're standing so deep?' Ella replied, 'Bob, over here we just can't play the way you want us to play. It doesn't work.' I asked him why it didn't work, and he told me the turf was softer. I asked what that had to do with it. Ella explained that the softer ground meant he could not accelerate so rapidly. 'But neither can the defence,' I said. 'Surely that evens things out.' Ella said, 'Look, Bob, I don't know why, but it just doesn't work.' I told him that I thought he was wrong

Willie Ofahengaue . . . a player who is always part of the action.   Peter Bush

— that he ought to be playing the type of game that had made him successful in Australia. 'You're not playing any good,' I said to him. 'I'm watching you on television and you're looking ordinary. You play any way you like, but my advice to you is that how you played to get into the side is how you're going to succeed over there.' Ella ended up by saying he would think about it.

When the 1982 Wallabies accepted and conformed to my method of play, they must have felt they were taking a gamble. Times have changed. What was considered then a radical style of play fraught with danger is being adopted in a growing number of countries around the world as a standard which all players should aspire to. In Australia, it is widely played from the first-grade level upwards, and I am confident it will sooner or later filter down through the lower grades, as it did years ago at Randwick. Frankly, I take the view there is simply no other logical way to play openside, attacking Rugby.

The type of attacking strategy I have outlined does not work all the time, of course. In a typical Rugby match a team will get the ball perhaps 150 times, if second and third phases are counted, yet if it scores five tries it is considered to have done well. The success rate here is thus about one in thirty, which means that, even when a team is successful, roughly twenty-nine of every thirty attacking movements do not result in a try. The aim of the attacking team on those twenty-nine occasions should be to do things which will enable them to keep possession, because this will limit the opposition's opportunities to score. The policy has worked successfully for us. In Test matches in 1991 Australia scored thirty-five tries to five, and those Tests included three against New Zealand and two against England.

I do not suggest that the Australian team has been following my method of play to the letter. As much as I would desire it, this could never be possible, given the limited scope which a national coach has to work with his team. In the case of the 1991 Wallabies, there were other factors which made this specially difficult. In the first place, our mid-field consisted of Michael Lynagh, Tim Horan and Jason Little, all of whom come from Queensland, where the preferred style of Rugby has little in common with mine. None of these players conform naturally to the method of play I promote. Indeed, by background and inclination they are are about as far removed from it as it is possible to be. Yet these three and the fullback, Marty Roebuck, were the four in the Australian team who constructed the play. Roebuck does play for New South Wales, which leans more towards my concept than Queensland does, but before Roebuck joined the Australian team I hadn't had much contact with him, either.

I have read one or two Rugby writers in recent years who were critical of Michael Lynagh for kicking the ball too often. The suggestion was he was not conforming to my game plan. The truth is I never present the team

Michael Lynagh . . . his tactical kicking exposed a flaw in John Kirwan's play.

with a game plan as such. The team doesn't run on to the field with instructions to do this at a certain time or do that at another time. I am much more concerned with *how* players do things, rather than *what* they do. I tell the players that when they do this they should do it this way, and that when they do that they should do it that way, but by and large I leave it to them to decide what to do as various situations arise.

In any case, I am all in favour of kicking in certain situations or for certain reasons. By 1991 I had observed that John Kirwan had trouble catching a high ball that he had to run to, and we decided to try to capitalise on this weakness. This was kicking for a specific tactical purpose. We were not simply kicking to Kirwan. We were kicking a high ball that was so directed that he would have to run some distance to get under it. This strategy resulted in Rob Egerton scoring a converted try against the All Blacks at the Sydney Football Stadium in 1991. The kick is also an invaluable tool in moving defences around. Take the hypothetical case of an opposition which lined all its backs in flat formation across the field. It would obviously make sense to, say, kick the ball behind the open-side winger to push him back and so create space for us to move. The kick should never be an end in itself, however. It should be no more than a means of giving ourselves a better chance of attacking with the ball in hand. What I strongly oppose is the use of the kick as the *primary* means of getting the ball in front of the advantage line.

After the World Cup in 1991 one English writer, Steve Bale, presented what I considered a very perceptive appreciation of the Wallabies' play. In particular, he admired their understanding of how to do things in impromptu situations. He wrote in the *Independent*: 'Spectators will remember the occasionally dazzling Rugby, but for our coaches the lesson is far more profound: how to adopt and adapt the Wallabies' outstanding array of tactical options right from the specifics of individual moves for individual circumstances to the more general knowledge of what to do and how to do it in any given situation.' He was picking up here on the fact that the Australians knew how to react as each set of circumstances arose. They were conscious, whenever they did anything, of the effect it would have on the players around them.

The Australian team which came closest to achieving my concept of play in mid-field was the 1982 side. The backline then was Philip Cox, Mark Ella, Michael Hawker, Gary Ella, Roger Gould at fullback, and Peter Grigg and David Campese on the wings. I have no doubt that the present Michael Lynagh-Tim Horan-Jason Little mid-field combination is superior to its 1982 equivalent in all-round ability. Nevertheless, the Ella-Hawker-Ella combination lent itself to the type of game I was advocating, simply because these players had been exposed to it for a long time. Doing things under pressure is not easy. You cannot be successful at it unless it has been built into your make-up as a player. In the three days a national coach has with his team before a Test, he cannot hope to build it into a player's make-up. He may try to, but you can be sure that when the player comes under pressure in the match he will revert to doing things the way he has always done them.

So getting the team to play exactly as I would like it to play has not been easy. At times, we have chosen players in the Test side who were not physically the best players yet who had the technique and the mental wherewithal to do a specific job that had to be done. But this is a second-best option. Ideally, we should have players in the team who are both physically the best *and* strong in the mental and technique departments. In 1991 I felt we were moving in this direction. After the World Cup, the England player Rob Andrew wrote an article in which he complimented the Australian team. He concluded it by saying that, from an Englishman's point of view, the frightening thing was that the Wallabies were likely to get better. He recognised that the team had a great deal of untapped potential. This is true. The best performances of the World Cup Wallabies are yet to come.

I have been asked how close the Wallabies came in the World Cup to playing what I consider ideal Rugby. I reply that they did not come as close to it as in Australia earlier in the year. We played extremely well against England in Sydney in 1991. Indeed, I would say the England match was our best performance of the year. I did think we played extremely well in the first half of the match against the All Blacks in the World Cup semi-final, but by and large in the World Cup we did not reach the high standards we set in Australia a few months before.

Some teams, I have observed, do not actually try to win a match until they have lost it. You will often see a team doing all the things a Rugby team is supposed to do on the field but doing them without a single, specific purpose in mind. Sure, if opportunities to score come along it will take them, but its primary motivation is not a positive, aggressive desire to score. Later in the match, when the players look at the scoreboard and see they are perhaps 12 points behind with only fifteen minutes to go, they start throwing the ball around. Suddenly, they are playing with the objective of scoring, but by then it may be too late.

We have all known of teams which were trailing their opponents badly well into the second half but then staged a dramatic fightback, scoring two or three tries in a matter of minutes and grabbing victory on the final whistle. What really happens in most of these cases, I suggest, is that the team which is behind starts to play well because it no longer feels it has anything to lose. The team is not fighting back as such, it is just playing differently. The players say to themselves, 'The game is virtually lost. We can afford to take risks. So why not give it a shot?' The question I pose is why wait until the match is all but lost before taking risks and giving it a shot? Why not give it a shot when the score is nil-all? Here lies, in my opinion, the real test of courage in Rugby. It requires no courage at all for a team which is behind and has nothing to lose to start taking risks. Most 'brave fightbacks' you hear about were not brave at all. Quite the opposite. The team with real courage is the one which has something to lose and yet is prepared to take risks.

THE TOP JOB

In 1977, my first year as coach, Randwick had made the Sydney grand final. Next year the prospects looked even brighter. We had some fine players who had come up from Colts the year before, players such as Bruce Malouf and Greg McElhone, who were all a year older and stronger. There were other promising players straight out of school, including the Ella brothers, Tony Walsh and Dave Ramsey. We still had good players from the previous year such as Adrian Jones, John Hoare and Ken Wright. In twenty matches in 1978 we scored ninety-nine tries and 606 points, which meant we averaged five tries and thirty points a game. We went on to win the Sydney premiership. It was Randwick's first win since 1974.

The Ella brothers fitted into the pattern of play I was developing at Randwick very easily. To some extent this was because they were already familiar with it. Their coach at Matraville High, Geoff Mould, had been strongy influenced by Cyril Towers in his Rugby thinking. In other words, the Ellas had simply been listening to the same tune played by another instrument. There is no doubt that their exceptional skill was a significant factor in the success of Randwick over the next few years, although it is also true that Randwick has continued to be successful since they left.

The 1981 side was probably the strongest Randwick team I have seen. We played a powerful Manly side in the grand final and thrashed it. We were leading well into the second half when Lloyd Walker had to go off injured and, partly out of sympathy, I brought on Dave Ramsey, who had been out with a broken shoulder and was still carrying the injury. I felt that he deserved a run in the final match of the season. Manly's Mitchell Cox took advantage of the situation to run in two late tries, which gave the Manly score some respectability. I have not seen a Sydney club play more accurate and more controlled football than Randwick did in 1981. The forward pack may not have been as formidable as the Randwick forward pack in the early 1990s, but its backline was superb. In fact, I am quite sure Randwick's fourth-grade backline in 1981 was better, technically, than any other first-grade backline in the competition.

One of the advantages of the backline strategy I had introduced at Randwick was that it enabled players with limited physical ability to outplay opponents who were superior physically. Lloyd Walker is a player who comes to mind here. Nobody would suggest that Walker is particularly well-equipped physically, yet I would argue there has never been a more influential player in club Rugby in Australia. He is, above all, a player who attacks the advantage line. To simply say he has good peripheral vision is to understate his extraordinary awareness of what is happening around him. He does not merely have 180 degree vision, it has often seemed to me, but 360 degree vision.

Walker did play for Australia and scored for Australia, but he would have achieved more if he had been blessed with more confidence and had made himself fitter. By comparison, Mark Ella trained very hard. The popular view was that Ella was a lazy trainer, and I think Mark liked to promote that idea of himself, because it somehow added to the myth. It was not true. When we were touring France in 1983 we did special fitness tests on all the players, who were then graded in various levels. Only three forwards and one back made the top level. The forwards were Mark McBain, Simon Poidevin and Steve Tuynman, and the back was Mark Ella.

Randwick's grand final victory in 1981 meant I had now coached the team to three successive Sydney premierships. By this time an ambition to coach the Australian side had begun stirring within me. I was convinced that the type of game I had coached Randwick to play successfully at the club level could be played successfully at the international level, and I was eager for a chance to prove it. Another thing which encouraged me to stand for the top job was that Mark Ella had begun to develop a style of play in the Australian team which was certainly contrary to the type of game I wanted him to play at Randwick, and I could see this was seriously reducing his effectiveness as a player. I have already recounted how I phoned him while he was touring Britain with the Wallabies in 1981 to ask why he was standing so deep. I found it hard to accept his explanation that the softer turf in Britain made it impossible for him to play in the way he played for Randwick. I thought to myself after I put down the phone, 'Surely he can't honestly believe that.'

I accept that it is normal for a player to amend his style of play to suit the needs of the team he is playing for and the coach he is playing under. When you see a player deprived of the very key to his success, however, you feel compelled to act. There are two possibilities in such a case. One is that the player's special strengths have not been recognised. The other is that his strengths have been recognised, but that a conscious decision has been taken not to let him use them. Either way, it was rather unfortunate for Mark Ella.

I am not suggesting my concern about Mark Ella was the main factor in my deliberations about the national coaching job, but it was a factor. I was asked to make myself a candidate by a number of Rugby people in New South Wales. They told me they believed it was in the best interests of Australian Rugby for me to do so and they promised me their support if I did. So I decided to stand. At the time, there had been talk in the media by David Lord and others about an alleged split between Queensland and New South Wales players on the recent tour of Britain. The players denied this vehemently, and on the basis of my own experience with touring sides I doubt very much whether such a split occurred. What may have happened is that a number of senior players who were close friends spent a lot of time together, for I know such a grouping did exist at that time. In any event, this alleged split between the players was cited as one reason for a change of coach.

I was duly elected. I do not know for sure, but I understand I received all five of New South Wales' votes and neither of Queensland's two votes. The first person to phone me after my appointment was announced was the man I was replacing, Bob Templeton. He congratulated me and offered me his support, which I appreciated very much.

In recent years Bob and I have discussed how and why various people have won and lost the national coaching job over the years. Before I lost the job in 1984 there had been what I considered an underhand campaign to erode my support. Essentially, this campaign consisted of feeding misinformation to the Rugby officials who were to vote. In the light of this experience, I asked Bob Templeton one day if any similar campaign of misinformation had been directed against him before he lost the job to me in 1982. Bob said yes, there had been. Word had been spread that the players were unhappy with him as coach and that by showing favouritism to certain players he had split the team. When Bob told me this, I said to

Whatever Bob Templeton and I are laughing about here, it wasn't the 1982 voting for the Australian coach's job for which I displaced him.

Mark Baker, John Fairfax Group

him at once that I wanted him to know I'd had no knowledge of such a campaign and was certainly not a party to it. In fact, the possibility of it had not even occurred to me until I became a victim of the same kind of thing.

Bob Templeton has worked closely with me in recent years as assistant coach, and I am pleased to say he and I have remained good friends. I have stood against him and against Jeff Sayle for coaching jobs in the past and beaten both of them. Afterwards, both have promised me total support and loyalty, and both have proved to be as good as their word. This reveals, I believe, a rare quality of character. Templeton coached Queensland for more than twenty years, an enormously long span for anyone in such a job. He has absorbed such a vast quantity of knowlege about Rugby that I consider him an irreplaceable resource. This is why I asked him to become my assistant coach in 1988. Players in the present Australian team have told me that Templeton's presence somehow makes them feel in touch with Australian teams of the past — that they are part of a proud tradition which they must live up to. Templeton is also a living symbol of the game's international dimension. Everybody in Rugby, everywhere, knows Bob Templeton.

It goes without saying that Templeton and I have very different approaches to the game. We both want to get the ball in front of our forward pack. The essential difference between us is that I prefer the ball to be carried there by hand, whereas Tempo generally preferred to have it kicked there. Rightly or wrongly, it was largely because of this difference, I believe, that I was chosen national coach in his place. There was a feeling abroad that Australia needed to play a different kind of game, that it ought to be playing more in the 'Australian style,' although precisely what that term means I have never quite understood. I do know that many Rugby officials believed — or at least perceived the Rugby public to believe — that Australia should be playing a so-called running game, rather than a kick-and-chase game.

Whether or not my type of game is superior to the other, there is no doubt it is the more popular. In 1984, when it became clear I was in danger of being toppled, the *Sydney Sun* conducted a telephone poll to try to find out whom the public preferred as coach. The result was Dwyer 360 votes and Alan Jones thirteen. A joke went around Rugby circles later: 'Which two Manly players didn't vote for Jones?'

I was never popular with everyone, of course. After I was appointed Australian coach, the Rugby writer for the *Courier Mail* newspaper in Brisbane, Frank O'Callaghan, wrote an article under the heading 'Bob Who?' Not long afterwards I was at Ballymore, and O'Callaghan came up to introduce himself to me. 'I'm Frank O'Callaghan,' he said, to which I could not resist replying, 'Frank who?' Unfortunately, this went right over Frank's head. I don't often come up with retorts as sharp as this one, so I was sorry it went unnoticed.

7

BOOS AT BRISBANE

When I reflect on it now, I find it strange how the fortunes of two players, Paul McLean and Mark Ella, were so closely entwined with my own as I began my career as Australian coach. At that time there was a strong undercurrent of debate over how the position of five-eighth ought to be played and who should play it, Ella or Paul McLean. The annual Australian club championship between the winners of the Sydney and Brisbane competitions actually owes its existence to this debate. It happened that some Randwick supporters and some supporters of McLean's club in Brisbane, Brothers, had been arguing about which of the two players was superior. The only way to settle the issue, they decided, was to pit one five-eighth against the other in a Randwick-Brothers match, and one of the Brothers supporters, Bernie Power, the man who went on to launch Powers Beer, put up a trophy. It happened that Randwick and Brothers had been the winners of their respective premier-ships the year before, 1981, and what started out as a one-off match became an annual fixture between the premier clubs.

That inaugural match in 1982 was played in Brisbane, which for us was an obvious disadvantage. Another disadvantage was that Brothers had played two competition matches, whereas Randwick had not even played a trial match. To make things worse, the match was played in intense heat, which, presumably, the Brisbane players were more accustomed to. Yet Randwick won fairly comfortably, mainly because of the superiority of our forwards. Our much-vaunted backline did not perform so well, which could probably be attributed to the fact that backs tend to be touch players who take one or two matches to find form. One memory of the match that lives with me is of the Brothers flanker Tony Shaw hitting Mark Ella in the throat with a late flying elbow, a blow which damaged Ella's larynx. I don't know if the blow was deliberate or not. If it was deliberate, I think Ella would have been entitled to resent it. After all, Shaw and Ella played together in the Test side and, in fact, had been touring Britain together

Paul McLean . . . a player whose talent never quite managed to reach full bloom.   Mike Brett

with the Wallabies a few months before. A blow to the throat is not what you normally expect of a team-mate.

As a test of the relative merits of Ella and McLean, the match was inconclusive. McLean could not excel because his forwards received a drubbing, and Ella did not excel because Randwick's entire backline was not functioning. McLean was a very fine Rugby player and a very fine athlete. He had excellent hand skills and foot skills, and he was also a much faster runner than most people gave him credit for. Before a seven-a-side match between Randwick and Brothers in Brisbane I remember warning Mark Ella to keep a close eye on McLean, saying that once he got away there was no way Ella would catch him. Ella was sceptical about this, but his brother Glen agreed with me. 'You won't catch him, Mark,' he said. As fullback, Glen had had personal experience of McLean's speed.

I viewed McLean as a player whose talent never quite managed to reach full bloom. I had the impression that he was somehow restricted, that there were hidden shackles preventing him displaying the full range of his abilities. Perhaps it was the five-eighth position itself which restricted him. In my opinion it is a pity to position a good athlete like McLean at five-eighth, because many of his talents must necessarily be wasted. Five-eighth is a restricted position. I am not suggesting that it is actually a disadvantage to be a good athlete if you are playing at five-eighth, but the trouble is good athletes tend to want to exercise all their athleticism, and the five-eighth position does not allow them to. Darren Junee, who has played at five-eighth, is a good example of such an athlete. He is a natural runner who wants to run. Brett Papworth was another. We did look at the possibility of putting McLean on the wing. I sometimes wondered, too, how successful he might be at outside-centre.

If I had reservations about McLean as a player, they were based entirely on tactical and positional grounds. A five-eighth's primary function is to draw defence and so open up space for the runners outside him. I always tell my mid-field players — five-eighth, inside-centre and outside-centre — that the more times they are tackled in a match the better. This is true even if they are tackled with the ball, for they will be still be restricting the scope of operation of the opposition's defence. The type of kicking game which Paul McLean grew accustomed to playing at five-eighth did not, in my view, satisfy the requirements of the position. To play this type of game he needed to give himself room, and by giving himself room he ensured that he did not absorb any defence. As soon as I see a five-eighth move around into that 'first slip' or 'second slip' position, which McLean liked to occupy, I know his team has a problem. Some five-eighths end up almost in a wicketkeeper's position. Michael Hawker used to place himself behind the scrum like this when he wanted to kick, which meant automatically that his team was incapable of attacking. Where the five-eighth ought to stand is at 'extra gully'.

Many people, especially Queenslanders, held me personally responsible for the exclusion of McLean and Roger Gould, both Queenslanders, in the first Test against Scotland in 1982. It was my first Test as coach, and Australia lost. The record needs to be set straight on a couple of matters here. First, Gould was not *dropped* at all. You have to be a current member of the team before you can be dropped, and Gould was not a current member. He had been dropped from the last Test on the Wallabies' tour of Britain in 1981, the most recent Australia had played, a selection I obviously had nothing to do with. Second, Mark Ella did not replace McLean as five-eighth. He simply retained the position he occupied in that previous Test. McLean had played in that Test, but as fullback, not five-eighth.

With hindsight, I am prepared to admit that the team for that Test could have been better chosen. It was the first Australian side I had helped select, and the other selectors, John Bain and Bob Templeton, were willing to give me, as coach, some scope in the choice of players I felt I needed. They were not willing to let me choose the team by myself, however. There is nothing unusual about this. I was first appointed an Australian selector in 1982, yet it was not until 1991 that an Australian team was chosen which I entirely agreed with, and I am referring here both to touring squads and Test XVs. The reason it finally happened in 1991 wasn't that the other selectors let me have my way. It was simply that for once the majority view of the selectors coincided with my own.

Since that 1982 Test in Brisbane I have been asked hundreds of times to reveal whether I was primarily reponsible for leaving McLean and Gould out. I have never answered the question, because it would be ethically wrong of me to do so. I do concede the team we chose was a bit of a hotchpotch. It was some of this, some of that, and all of nothing. This is always a possibility when three or more people sit down to choose anything. I know of an Australian coach who, according to rumour, was actually the third choice of the council making the appointment. Some of them wanted A, others wanted B and, being unable to agree, they voted in C.

Looking back on that 1982 Test, I fear that I tried to go too far too soon. I tried to alter things too drastically. At Randwick, my main contribution to the team's success was to improve its forward play, not its backline play. Randwick's forwards have been a key factor in the club's success ever since I became Randwick coach. In fact, the forwards have been *the* key factor in recent years. I certainly did not neglect the forwards in their preparation for that Test, as a few people have suggested. If anything, I spent more time with the forwards than with the backs. In the event, our forwards played a timid game and came off a poor second best. They even lost a defensive scrum against the head, as a result of which Scotland scored a converted try. There were other mistakes. On two occasions players failed to pass the ball to an unmarked player. In one case the unmarked player was Glen Ella and in the other Michael O'Connor. Each would certainly have scored a try if he had received the ball. It was therefore wrong to suggest, as various people with their own agendas did suggest afterwards, that the cause of our defeat was our failure to kick goals in the absence of Paul McLean.

I do agree Australia may have fared better in that Test if we had chosen Gould as fullback instead of Glen Ella. This was not because Gould necessarily deserved to be chosen ahead of Ella. Rather, it was because of the intense hostility directed at Ella by the Brisbane crowd, which, I believe, had a very negative effect on him during the match. Mark Ella told me later that being conscious of this he felt under pressure throughout the match to do things which involved Glen. One of our pre-planned moves ended with Mark passing the ball to Glen. The move came off, Glen had a gap in front of him, but Mark threw the pass so hard it nearly knocked Glen over. Mark very rarely made an error like this, and I am sure he did it then because he was overly anxious to ensure Glen scored a try. The reception Glen Ella received from the crowd and also from the Brisbane media was disgraceful. Glen was booed when he ran on to the field, and he was jeered repeatedly early in the game. Michael O'Connor has since

Roger Gould and Glen Ella, rival candidates for the test fullback berth in 1982. Choosing Ella to play at Ballymore incurred the hostility of the Queensland crowd. John Fairfax Group

described this as the most unpleasant moment he has known in sport. I should have foreseen it, but I didn't, and that was my mistake.

After the match one of the Ballymore seat-holders came up to me and told me that I was a traitor to my country. I was so angered by the remark that the team's manager, Chilla Wilson, who was there, saw a need to restrain me physically. When I go to Ballymore I still sometimes see the individual who insulted me that day, and after all these years the memory of it still disgusts me. I find it astonishing that someone with such an attitude would even want to attend a Rugby match.

At the time the Queensland members on the Australian Rugby Union were Lyn Crowley and Norbert Byrne. Crowley said to me later that he would never forgive me for what he perceived to be *my* selection for that Test. I have no doubt that lingering hostility among Queenslanders influential in Rugby was a factor in my losing the national coaching job two years later.

As a final comment on this whole controversy, I must say that what

Michael Hawker and Peter Grigg, who came back into the Australian team for the second Test against Scotland in 1982. Peter Bush

aggravates me more than anything when I am criticised for team selections is the suggestion, implicit in a lot of this criticism, that I pick the wrong players *knowing* them to be the wrong players. Many critics seem to imply this — that I know perfectly well A is the ideal halfback for the Australian team but because I like B personally or perhaps because B plays for Randwick I choose B instead. Do the people who suggest this really believe a coach would not pick what he considered the best team when his own reputation was on the line? Do they think there is any coach, anywhere, who doesn't want desperately to win? The idea insults the intelligence.

McLean and Gould both returned to the side for the second Test against Scotland at the Sydney Cricket Ground. Michael Hawker was moved into his normal centre position and the two Ella brothers and Andrew Slack were left out. The Test was played in heavy rain on an unusually cold day, and I have a memory of O'Connor doing sprints across the ground at half-time to keep warm. During training for the match I reminded McLean there were ways of getting the ball across the advantage line other than by kicking it. I suggested that if he found prospects looking unpromising on the open side he should work the blind side. With this in mind, we practised three or four blind-side moves by the backs on the day before the Test. McLean carried out the plan superbly, and we scored several tries from these blind-side moves. Australia won the Test by 33 to 9, a then record score for Australia against a first-class Rugby nation.

After the match I was interviewed by Frank O'Callaghan of the Brisbane *Courier Mail*, and in a spirit of generosity I told him that the players won the game themselves and that I could not take any credit for the victory. For once, Frank was happy to take me at my word. Frank had always seemed to doubt everything I told him, but now he was prepared to accept absolutely that I deserved no credit at all, and reported this fact widely. I learned then that humility in public never pays.

8

A TEAM OF UNKNOWNS

On the night of the second Test against Scotland in 1982, ten of Australia's leading players delivered statements to the chairman of national selectors, announcing that for personal and business reasons they would not be available for the tour of New Zealand which was to follow. Nine of the players had played in the Test that afternoon, and all were from Queensland. They included some of the best and most experienced players in Australia at the time, men of the calibre of Paul McLean, Brendan Moon, Mark Loane and Tony Shaw. The tenth player was Gary Pearse of New South Wales, who did not play in the Test that day.

The news shocked me. I had been reasonably close to several of the players who pulled out — or so I thought — but I had not heard as much as a whisper of their intentions. Suddenly, on the eve of the announcement of the touring side for New Zealand, the heart of our team had been ripped out. I have very disjointed memories of the few hours of turmoil that followed. One is of talking to Michael O'Connor's father in the corridor outside the home side's dressing room in the Members Pavilion at the Sydney Cricket Ground, near the entrance to the bar. O'Connor's father was unhappy about his son's decision to withdraw. I gathered that he had tried to talk Michael out of it but had failed. This was a disappointment for me, and it was also a pity for Australian Rugby as a whole, because O'Connor followed up his withdrawal by switching to Rugby League the following season. He was a very talented player, and I was sorry to see him go.

The players who pulled out said in explanation of their decision that they had been playing too much Rugby. They had played a heavy home season the year before, they had gone on a long tour of Britain in the off-season and they had just played two tough Tests at home against Scotland. Now, they faced the prospect of lining up for an arduous tour of New Zealand, a country they had toured before and did not particularly want

Michael O'Connor, one of the ten players who declared themselves
unavailable to tour New Zealand in 1982. He later switched to rugby
league.   Mike Brett

to tour again.

Many people suspected there was more to it than that. It was widely believed that most of the players were withdrawing from the touring side in protest at my replacement of Bob Templeton as coach. My own view is that this was probably a factor in the decisions taken by most of the ten players. I doubt very much if it was the only factor, however. Several players, including Mark Loane and Michael O'Connor, assured me later that their withdrawal had nothing whatever to do with who was coach, yet I remain to be convinced that this was the case generally. In any event, it was an appallingly thoughtless action for sportsmen in their position to take. I did not object to their withdrawing, for it was naturally within their rights for them to do that, but rather to the timing of it.

It was generally assumed that the players had delayed making the announcement until after the Sydney Test in case it jeopardised their chances of being selected for the Test. I do not know whether this is true or not, but if it was true the players would stand condemned of gross selfishness. It would mean they put their desire to play in one more Test ahead of the desire of other players to go on the New Zealand tour. In my view, this was the worst feature of the whole affair. There were various fringe players who might have been chosen to go on the tour if we had had time to properly assess them. In a few cases, probably, this would have been their first and last chance of touring with the Wallabies. They were denied it, however, by the decision of the ten players to withdraw at the last minute.

In any case, it is most unlikely that any of the nine players would have jeopardised his place in the Test team that day by withdrawing from the tour earlier. The selectors then, as now, had a policy of choosing the best team for the match in question. A player was either available for the match or he wasn't. Only in cases where the selectors had trouble choosing between two players might they have taken availability for a future tour into account. The proper course of action would have been for one of the players, probably the captain, to have come to me or one of the other selectors and asked to discuss the matter, because I am sure he would have been given an assurance along these lines. It is sad that this did not happen.

Because of the late withdrawals, the national selectors were placed in the bizarre situation of having to phone around on the day the team was to be chosen, asking various players if they might be available. To appreciate the nature of problem we selectors were presented with, you must understand that before a touring side is chosen the selectors compile a list of candidates, each of whom is examined closely and evaluated. The fact that as many as ten players withdrew meant that to replace them we suddenly had to consider players we had barely looked at before. This is why we had to find out first which players were available. One player who would certainly have made the tour as a replacement was John Maxwell, but unfortunately for us he had signed a lease on his business premises only a week before. His wife, Jennifer, tried to talk John into going anyway, but he decided it was impossible. This was a pity, because Maxwell was a fine player over many years and would have been an asset in New Zealand.

At times, our search for players became almost farcical. We were in need of a tight-head prop, and there was no obvious candidate for the position. I did know of a loose-head prop who I thought might do the job, provided he'd had a reasonable amount of experience playing tight-head, so I phoned his club coach to ask about him. I explained to the coach that I had seen this player perform in trials and I knew he was primarily a loose-head prop, but I was hoping that he might also have played tight-head and done it successfully, because we were keen to have a prop who could play both sides. The coach replied that his man had played tight-head prop many times with great success. He was sure he would be ideal for us. I must have detected something in his voice which made me suspicious, because I said to him, 'Look, if you're having me on, I will never speak to you again. This is a serious question I'm asking, and your answer will have serious consequences. Now tell me again: has this bloke ever played tight-head prop?' There was a moment's pause, and the coach said, 'I've never seen him play tight-head prop.' The player was not chosen.

The tight-head props we ended up taking were John Griffiths and Andy McIntyre. Griffiths was past his best and was somewhat out of condition. He was still extremely powerful, but he frequently broke down at training. I think that if someone had got hold of Griffiths when he was younger and made him concentrate on his fitness he might have become an outstanding player, for he was certainly very strong and was technically without peer. His problem, I gather, was that he played Rugby in his best years in Western Australia, where he did not have to train hard, being much better than anyone else. Eventually, he snapped an achilles tendon under the duress of training, and Stan Pilecki, one of the players who had previously withdrawn, made himself available to come over as replacement.

Our other tight-head prop, Andy McIntyre, went on to become a fixture in the Australian front row in the 1980s. When we chose McIntyre for the tour he was not even first choice for Queensland. In fact, McIntyre played quite a few Tests before he became Queensland's first choice in the position. Another forward who had the door opened for him on that tour was Steve Cutler. Thus, two great players of the future, McIntyre and Cutler, who would otherwise probably not have made the tour, were given their first chance in international Rugby.

Mark Ella had not even been in the Test side the day before. Now, he suddenly found himself captain of the touring Wallabies. I know many people felt Andrew Slack should have got the captaincy, but with our tour strategies already in disarray I felt I needed a leader who understood and felt confident with the type of game I wanted the team to play. It was to

One player who grabbed his chance in New Zealand in 1982 and went on to become a fixture in the Wallaby front row - Andy McIntyre.   _{Mike Brett}

Slack's great credit that at a team dinner on the last night of the tour he stood up and congratulated Ella. He said that at the outset of the tour he knew of Ella's great skills as an attacking player. He realised now what a hard worker Ella was and what a pillar of strength he was when the going got tough.

Ella was crucial to my plans. At that time there was a good deal of resistance among Australian players to the type of game I had been coaching at Randwick. Most of them knew about this style of play, but the Australian forwards, in particular, players like Mark Loane and Tony Shaw, wanted to have nothing to do with it. They did not understand it, so they dismissed it altogether. I find this kind of closed-mind attitude disappointing. I am a great believer in being prepared to listen whenever someone wants to tell me something. I may not always agree with what is

Mark Loane . . . wanted nothing to do with my type of game. Peter Bush

said and I may not remember it later, but I'm always happy to listen to it.

Long afterwards, Mark Loane made a comment to me which I thought was interesting. 'We probably did you a big favour by pulling out in 1982,' he told me. 'You were better off without a mob of narrow-minded players who wouldn't have wanted to go along with your type of play anyway.'

The tour was more successful than any of us dreamt it might be. By the end of the second Test, three-quarters of the way through the tour, we had lost only one match, and that was the first Test. Our victories in some of the provincial matches were overwhelming. Later, our performances fell away, perhaps because we felt we had already achieved more than anyone expected us to achieve and therefore relaxed a little. We lost three of the last four matches. Considering that we had set off with a team of virtual unknowns, the tour as a whole had to be judged hugely successful. The team we defeated in the second Test was a particularly strong New Zealand side — indeed, one of the strongest I have seen. Its forward pack consisted of Gary Knight, Andy Dalton and John Ashworth in the front row, Gary Whetton and Andy Haden in the second row (although Whetton did get dropped) and Murray Mexted, Mark Shaw and Graham Mourie in the back row — all legendary names. It was a great side with a great captain, Mourie, and it will be to the eternal credit of the 1982 Wallabies that we defeated it.

The New Zealanders were stunned when we won that second Test. They could not understand how a makeshift team we had scraped together at the last moment could possibly have managed it. The final score, 19-16, flattered New Zealand. In the second half we attacked their line time after time and did not get a single penalty. David Campese scored a gem of a try, running off a flat backline. At the press conference I gave after the match I noticed that Mourie stayed to listen. Someone said to me later that

Euphoria at Athletic Park after defeating the All Blacks in the second test of the '82 series. The happy chappies are Peter Grigg, Roger Gould, Mark Ella and David Campese.   Peter Bush

Mourie's presence was a sure sign that the New Zealanders were intrigued by how we had achieved a seemingly impossible victory.

Between the second and third Tests we began to notice the same faces appearing among the spectators who came along to watch our practice sessions, and we were sure they were spies. We therefore spent a lot of time practising things we weren't going to do in the Test and not much time on things we were going to do. I had been looking closely at the New Zealand defensive pattern and saw what seemed an opportunity to beat it. I decided to use a double cut-out play. The five-eighth would cut out the inside-centre and pass directly to the outside-centre, and the outside-centre would cut out the fullback, who by now had joined the backline, and pass directly to the winger, and finally the winger would pass to the fullback, now looping around him. As we went into the third Test I gave the players instruction to attempt this move from the kick-off. The move came off, and Roger Gould scored in the corner. After two minutes we were ahead 6 points to nil. It had all gone so precisely to plan that Stan Pilecki, sitting on the reserve bench in front of me, turned around and said, 'What did you say to do next?'

Towards the end of the first half Steve Williams went over the line at the end of a movement which had begun at the far end of the field, but the referee ruled there had been a forward pass three or four players earlier. That try, if converted, would have taken us to a lead of 18 to 6 and, I think, would have been the winning of the match. New Zealand was playing an ultra-controlled game. The ball was rarely allowed to go beyond the inside-centre, Bill Osborne, who kept charging up and giving it back to the forwards. Osborne was injured at one point in this match and went to leave the field but was recalled by the captain, Graham Mourie. A story went around later that Osborne told Mourie he could not run, and Mourie replied, 'You won't have to run. Just don't pass it.' New Zealand had a penalty goal before half-time, so instead of going into the break with a lead of 12 points we led by only three, which was never going to be enough. New Zealand won the match 33 to 18.

So we lost the series, but it was a marvellous tour in every respect. We arranged plenty of social and recreational activities, and I think everyone had a great time. The players even found the training to be fun. I remember Andrew Slack saying to me, with some surprise, that for once he enjoyed coming to training because it was interesting and stimulating. I was encouraged to hear him say so.

The press in New Zealand could not have praised us more. They had marvelled at our running style of play, and I think they had admired our skill generally. Writing in a poetic vein, the New Zealand journalist Terry McLean said: 'Bravo the Wallabies! On their day they lit such a fire as by God's grace shall never be put out in the subsequent history of New Zealand Rugby.' We could not have returned to Australia any happier.

9

CAMPESE

David Campese came into his own on the tour of New Zealand in 1982. I am not sure whether he would have made the tour if Brendan Moon and the others had not pulled out, but even if he had he would have been a borderline choice and might have remained on the fringe of the team for much of the tour. Instead, he occupied centre-stage and performed brilliantly. Before the tour I knew next to nothing about him, which, I suppose, is an indication of how backward we were then in talent identification. A few months earlier Campese had played for the Australian under-21s against the Fijian under-21s in a curtain-raiser to the first Test against Scotland at Brisbane, and he had cut the Fijian defence to shreds. I asked at once who he was and was told he was a rising star in the Canberra competition. Then I saw him play a second time in the curtain-raiser to the second Test, and again he was brilliant in attack. It was obvious that here was a player of unusual potential, but I certainly did not mark him down as someone liable to break into the Test side. Although Moon had withdrawn, two other wingers of proven ability were going on the New Zealand tour, Peter Grigg and Mick Martin.

Campese played in a couple of the early tour matches, and as we approached the first Test a few of the senior players tried to advance his cause by telling me how much they admired him. 'How about the young bloke on the wing,' they would say. 'He's killing them.' By this time I was certainly looking at Campese as a contender for the Test side, and I think the other wingers must have seen him as a contender, too, because I noticed they were working extremely hard, doing sprints after training and so on. Campese saw them doing this and, perhaps believing he could not let them get an edge on him, he began joining them. Even then he was a very confident individual on the football field, although it was a confidence he kept within himself.

We picked him for the first Test, and on the very first occasion he touched a ball in Test Rugby he found himself opposed one-on-one by Stu

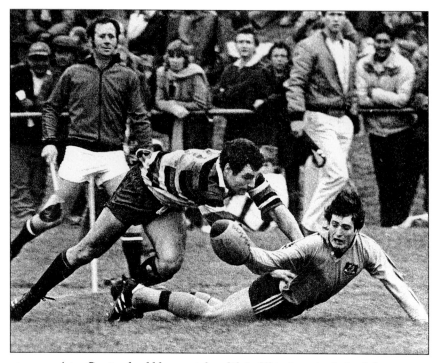

A try Campo should have got, but didn't. This shove in the back from Counties' old campaigner Alan Dawson, which went unpenalised, cost Campo the try and the Wallabies the match, at Pukekohe on the 1982 tour of New Zealand. Peter Bush

Wilson, then widely rated the number-one winger in the world, in the middle of Lancaster Park. Campese stood Wilson up and ran around him so easily that he might have been playing Test Rugby for years. He did it once or twice again before the match was over and on one occasion scored a try. I was enthused, and so was the media. They wrote of him in glowing terms next day.

That was a long time ago now, and I have seen a great deal of Campese in the meantime, but I don't believe I have ever lost the sense of wonder at his ability which I felt when I saw him run around Stu Wilson on Lancaster Park. I have tried to analyse him in all his achievements, and I have come to the conclusion that his greatest single asset is courage. Campese has always been willing to take a chance to achieve the best. He has never wanted to be restricted by the fear of failure, and by and large he has not been restricted. I have seen him hesitate, and I suppose this could be attributed to a fear of failure, but this has happened only rarely. His instinct is always to do things which are above the ordinary. The safe option may be to kick the ball thirty metres and put it into touch. Campese

David Campese . . . a heaven-made rugby player.   Garry Taylor knows that if he hits it just right he can kick a long ball which will go fifty metres and roll another twenty and perhaps put the opposition under pressure. The second option is invariably the one he will take.

Most players of flair, after they have been criticised many times for the mistakes they make, tend to withdraw into their shell as they get older. The audacity of youth tends to get worn down pretty quickly by hard experience. Mercifully, this has not happened with Campese. I think it did start to happen with Mark Ella, which is why I was eager to become Australian coach. I wanted to say to Ella: 'Don't listen to them, Mark — you can do it if you want to.'

I once attended a coaching conference which was addressed by the great Irish flyhalf and centre Mike Gibson. Gibson spoke about midfield play and he singled out self-confidence as a quality midfield players needed to possess if they were to overcome their opponents and do what they had to do. The only thing worse than a lack of self-confidence, he said, was a misplaced self-confidence. Campese is blessed with an abundance of self-confidence, and it is not misplaced. Campese's self-confidence is backed by outstanding physical talents, the most important of which is explosiveness. He is a speedy runner without being a sprinter. I certainly do not believe he was ever super-fast over 100 metres. He has tremendous power, however, and amazing acceleration, which, according to the experts, he owes to the type of muscle fibres he was born with. He has great balance and great kicking skills. In short, he is a heaven-made Rugby player.

Campese's tries are a little like Don Bradman's centuries. Most were brilliant, but because there were so many of them they are not easy to single out. One Campese try which I do remember clearly was scored in the second Test against Argentina in 1983. Mark Ella picked up a loose ball in counter attack and passed it to Campese, who made a long run along the western touchline at the Sydney Cricket Ground, in front of the Members Pavilion. An Argentine defender had Campese well covered, but when he moved in to tackle him Campese did his famous goose-step. The change of pace deceived the Argentinian so comprehensively that he dived into touch, clutching thin air. The referee, the Welshman Clive Norling, was so impressed by this that he went up to Campese as soon as he had scored and told him it was the best try he had ever seen.

At the 1991 World Cup I heard of some All Blacks being rude to their own supporters when approached for an autograph or just for a shake of the hand. Happily, the Australians at the World Cup had a reputation for being friendly and approachable, and Campese has always set a fine example in this respect. After a match at Whangarei in New Zealand, he stayed on for the best part of an hour at the ground signing autographs, and by the end of it all he had given away his socks, football shorts and taping. Unfortunately, he had left his mouthguard in the pocket of his shorts, so an urgent bulletin was broadcast on radio and television that evening,

Campo . . . the entire rugby world should be grateful that he did not switch to league.
Mike Brett

appealing to the recipient of Campese's shorts to please return his mouthguard. Happily, it came back that same night.

In recent years Campese has indulged in a little showmanship from time to time. Nowadays you will sometimes see him laughing on the field, for instance. The young Campese did not do this. Early in his career he was very quiet and very serious for as long as the match lasted. I think he was greatly influenced by the Ellas. He admired them enormously and he looked to them for support and acknowledgement. He is still good friends with them. In some ways, I suppose, he and the Ellas saw themselves as kindred spirits, players who were not restricted by the laws of conservatism to doing the ordinary.

It was reported many times that he was on the verge of switching to Rugby League, and the entire Rugby world should be grateful this did not happen. It is interesting to speculate how successful he might have been if he had made the move. Rugby League is essentially a game for individuals, a game you can succeed at if you excel in one-on-one encounters. The good constructive player in Rugby, the player who is able to make an opportunity for a team-mate two or three passes away, cannot be assured of success in League, for the simple reason that his constructive skills are not in demand there. On this basis, I would expect Campese to be successful in League. Campese is not really a constructive player. At the start of his career he could barely throw a pass which anyone was capable of catching, and I remember saying to him once, 'Don't pass the ball, Campo — just keep it. We'll come and get it from you.'

The Sydney Rugby writer Spiro Zavos suggested in the *Sydney Morning Herald* that Campese might make a great attacking five-eighth. It was a novel suggestion, but I do not agree with it. Campese is not, as I said before, a constructive player. Significantly, he has sometimes run into the five-eighth's position from the blind wing with great effect — this is how he scored his try against the All Blacks in the World Cup semi-final — but this is essentially a shock tactic. Campese asked me a few years ago why I didn't play him at fullback. My answer was that if his position was winger he could play fullback as well, but if his position was fullback he could not play winger as well. By making him winger, he is able to use his talents in both positions.

Campese's ability to beat a player in a one-on-one situation is fantastic, and I am sure this would have guaranteed his success in League, where yardage is so important. I rate him the best broken-field runner I have seen. Michael O'Connor was a good broken-field runner, and so was Brett Papworth, but neither was up to Campese's standard in my view. He is a better-equipped player today than he was in 1982. The game itself has evolved since then, and in particular there have been important advances in defensive patterns and in the analysis of the opposition's strengths and weaknesses. The old Campese, by which I mean the Campese of the early 1980s, might have been found wanting in some respects in the game as it is played today. Physically, he is better than ever. He has been conscientious about his fitness. He trains as hard as anyone in the Australian team and he has a good diet. Altogether, he is a better player now than when he started.

Jack Gibson, the celebrated League coach in Sydney, said to me one day that he would love to have Campese in his team for three reasons. One, he was a brilliant attacker. Two, he was a good chaser of the ball. Three, he had a high work rate. The last of these is quite true, incidentally, although Campese rarely receives acknowledgement for it. I told Gibson I was surprised to hear him say this, because I knew how much emphasis he placed on defence. Campese is a good cover-defender, but if his game does have a deficiency it is in head-on defence, which is something Gibson would naturally have been aware of. I asked Gibson if he did not think Campese's limited ability in head-on defence would have presented a problem for him. He replied, 'No. I'd have got somebody else to take care of it.'

10

THE KNIVES ARE DRAWN

I began my second year as Australian coach, 1983, with reasonably high hopes. On the one hand, there had been a sizeable turnover of players. A number of those who had made themselves unavailable for the New Zealand tour in 1982 had retired or, in the case of Tony Darcy and Michael O'Connor, had gone over to Rugby League. On the other hand, the players who had performed well in New Zealand were back, and I was confident we could build on the successes we had there. We had a predictably big win over a United States team which had actually given a good account of itself in the lead-up matches. I had noticed in these matches that the American cover defence was intent on getting across to the winger, which meant it left huge holes inside. I told our players to try putting up a centre kick, which they did with resounding success. After the match one of the American officials said to me in a pronounced drawl, 'You guys were just sitting there waiting for us, weren't you? You had us played for suckers.' It is not often you hear candour like this from the other side. I may point out that this was another instance when I did instruct the team to kick, a perfectly legitimate tactic when it has the specific purpose of exposing deficiencies in the opposition's defence.

Our home series was against Argentina. We found ourselves sadly wanting in the front-row department. John Meadows had just returned to the game after an illness but was not yet up to playing at Test level. We chose Stan Pilecki as loose-head prop for the first Test in Brisbane, a position which, I was led to believe, he had often played in before and would be able to handle. Our tight-head prop was Declan Curran. As I quickly discovered when the match got under way, Pilecki was not skilled in the loose-head position and was unable to cope with a tough, boring-in, tight-head prop of the quality of Argentina's Topo Rodriguez. It also emerged that Curran was carrying a groin injury. As a result, the Argentinians were able to pulverise our front row and actually scored two push-over tries. Argentina won the Test, which for us was a disappointing result.

Stan Pilecki . . . had a torrid introduction to test rugby opposite Topo Rodriguez.   Mike Brett

The Argentinians were always hard to beat at home, but I don't believe even they really expected to win in Australia. Our choice of front-rowers probably cost us the match, and with the other selectors I bore the responsibility for this. If I had been as experienced then as I am now, I would have made sure that the information on which we based our selections was more reliable.

For the second Test in Sydney we brought Meadows back into the loose-head position. He was a shorter man than Pilecki and therefore better suited to countering Rodriguez's style of play. There was nothing new about this style of tight-head play. It had been in vogue many years before. Rodriguez was simply reviving it with awesome effectiveness. Pilecki moved over to the tight-head position, to which a player of his big, strong physique was much better suited. We won the Test well, although not without the help of a penalty try which was awarded against Argentina for a deliberate knock-on. A lone Argentine defender did knock down a pass, but we were maybe forty metres from the line at the time, so the decision by the Welsh referee, Clive Norling, seemed a little harsh. It appeared to break the spirit of the Argentinians. Ironically, after we lost the first Test I was asked by a journalist what I thought of Norling's refereeing. The journalist was obviously expecting me to say something derogatory, but instead I replied that it was the best refereeing I had seen. The journalist at first thought I was being sarcastic, but I insisted this was my view. I don't know whether my praise ever reached Norling's ears, but, if it did, it obviously did us no harm a week later.

There was an important sequel to this tour by Argentina — Topo Rodriguez's arrival in Australia in the following year. He was to play twenty-six Tests for Australia, and he was undoubtedly one of the keys to Australia's successes in the years that followed.

Later that year we made a tour of France, always a tough undertaking. One reason that tours of France tend to be tough is that the standard of Rugby there is universally high, which means that playing two matches a week for six weeks or more takes a heavy physical toll. Another reason is that a team's inability to communicate with the locals produces a feeling of isolation which is never conducive to a confident, relaxed approach to the games. Foreseeing this problem, the tour manager, Chilla Wilson, and I made a big effort to do what we called the 'tourist thing'. We did homework on the places we were to visit, noting the various tourist attractions the players could go to see, and we made sure we had guides whenever possible. The French authorities did provide us with a liaison officer, but to our astonishment he was unable to speak English. The French officials who chose him were either very stupid or very smart.

I love France. I love the variety of its countryside, I love its cities and villages, and I have no objection whatever to its food and wine. We were looked after well and entertained, and we all had a good time. In fact, Chilla Wilson and I actively encouraged the players to enjoy themselves in the hope that this would counter their feeling of isolation, which it probably did to some extent. The Rugby wasn't so enjoyable, however. We drew with France in the first Test and lost the second. It was a disappointing result, but not altogether a surprising one. France had a particularly strong team that year and had won the Five Nations title. Moreover, France is never easy to beat in France. Even today, Australia is yet to win a series there.

Mark Ella played out of character for much of the tour and, for that reason, was not nearly so effective. I strongly suspect that a number of

When in France behave like the French. That's what Wallaby manager Chilla Wilson and I appear to be doing during the first test in France in 1983.   Col Whelan

senior players with a conservative outlook had talked Ella out of playing his natural game. The Australian players appeared afraid to run the ball against the French. I think they felt that the French were so fast that if our players were tackled and lost possession in midfield their French counterparts would present a threat. An Australian team would never be overawed in the same way today, which I suppose is a measure of the progress Australian Rugby has made since then. In the first Test Mark did nothing but kick the ball. In fact, there must have been twelve occasions in the match when the ball was kicked by us over the dead-ball line. It was a miserable Test for us in every respect. Roger Gould could not do the goal-kicking because of an injury, so Campese had to do it instead, and Campo is not a goal-kicker of international class. We did not lose the Test, but I count that match among my least happy Rugby memories.

Mark Ella was outstanding in defence throughout the tour, but I have never seen him so far off his game in attack. When I hear him commenting now, as he sometimes does, about the Australian team kicking the ball too much, I wonder whether this is the same Mark Ella talking who kicked the leather off the ball in France in 1983. I never saw Mark play like that before or after, and I feel sure that one or more players must have influenced him to do so. About this time Ella was thinking seriously of accepting an offer to play Rugby League, and after we returned to Australia I spent a lot of time trying to talk him out of it.

The tour was important in the development of a number of players who were to make a big impact on Australian Rugby over the next few years. It was Tommy Lawton's first tour and he also played his first Test. Steve Tuynman played his first Test; Michael Lynagh had his first tour; and Jeff Miller had his first tour. I remember Michael Hawker telling me while we were in France about a good prospect back in Sydney who was playing scrum half for Sydney University, then a second division club. 'You ought to have a look at him,' Hawker said. 'I'm not saying he'd make a world XV tomorrow, but he's definitely a player of the future.' The halfback was Nick Farr-Jones.

During the tour of France I heard for the first time that there was a move afoot back in Australia to depose me as coach and install Alan Jones in my place. The knives, I was warned, were out. It was clear I was returning to an uncertain future when I arrived home in Australia.

*   *   *   *

Alan Jones distinguished himself in 1983 by coaching Manly to victory in the the Sydney competition. Manly beat Randwick narrowly in the grand final, thus ending an unbroken run of success by Randwick which I had begun in 1978. Curiously, Jones seems to associate me in some way with the Randwick team which his team defeated in 1983. At a dinner I attended some years later, Jones spoke of Manly's win in 1983 and thanked me for leaving Matt Burke out of Randwick's grand final team, his point being, I assume, that Burke was a fine player who might have made it harder for Manly to win. I was in no position to leave Burke or anyone else out of the Randwick team that year, for the obvious reason that I was not the coach. I coached Randwick to four premiership victories in a row, 1978 to 1981, but after I became Australian coach early in 1982 I naturally gave up the Randwick post. If I had coached Randwick in 1983, we would certainly not have gone into the grand final with four injured players, as Randwick unfortunately did on that occasion.

Still, Jones' team did win the premiership, and he rightly gained a lot of kudos from the victory. I knew him slightly before this. He was close to Ross Turnbull, at that time a powerful figure in the New South Wales Rugby Union, and in the early 1980s he was given the job of managing the New South Wales team. I happened to speak to him one day after it was announced that he intended standing for the Manly coaching position. In my naivety, I tried to talk him out of it. I told him he was doing a great job as New South Wales manager, that it was a most important job, and that I thought he should continue to do it. I think I also raised the prospect of his one day becoming manager of the Australian team, a job I thought he would naturally aspire to.

Jones stood for the job, won it and took Manly to the grand final. Until

Alan Jones . . . I was heart-broken after he took the Wallaby coach's job from me in 1984. Col Whelan

I received word during the tour of France in late 1983 that a campaign was under way to make him Australian coach in my place, it had never occurred to me that he might be a candidate for the national job. Given his lack of experience of coaching at a senior level, he was about the last person I had expected to challenge me.

After I returned from France, I spoke to Turnbull by phone. He told me that he and the other New South Wales delegates to the Australian Rugby Union Council, which appoints the coach, were thinking of not giving me their vote when I came up for re-election in February 1984, a few months later. When I asked why, he told me they were concerned about my connections with the Randwick club. He was referring here to the fact that I had decided to stand for the position of Randwick's club coach. This was an overseeing position which would not require me to actually coach a team, so I did not see it as conflicting with the national coaching job. Turnbull reminded me that the New South Wales Rugby Union had a policy of limiting all Rugby officials to one job each. If you were a club official, therefore, you were not allowed to be a state or national official as well.

I told Turnbull I was aware of this rule but did not realise it was being enforced so rigidly. 'After all,' I said, 'I do know of one case where it hasn't been enforced.' Turnbull asked me what I was referring to, and I said, 'Alan

Jones did two jobs last year. He was the manager of the New South Wales team and coach of Manly.' This seemed to set Turnbull back momentarily. He replied that maybe there had been some inconsistency there, but the rule was still the rule.

It was clear to me the die was cast. I would get none of the five New South Wales votes. This was not the end of it, however. There were seven other votes from other states, and if I could win even six of them I was confident of retaining the job, since the chairman would surely give his casting vote to the incumbent. I was optimistic about winning the five votes from the southern states. Turnbull had been lobbying them in support of Jones, but delegates from these states phoned me to say they had been unimpressed by the line Turnbull was pushing and that they intended to support me.

This left Queensland, which controlled two votes. It was obvious their two primary votes would go to Bob Templeton, who was again a candidate for the job. What I needed was their preference votes, so I phoned the two Queensland delegates to discuss the matter. The first, Norbert Byrne, said he would take on board everything I had said and would consider it. He admitted he had not intended supporting me, but now, having spoken to me, he had an open mind. The second Queensland delegate was Lyn Crowley, the man who told me after the Scotland Test in Brisbane in 1982 that he would never forgive me for that team selection. Crowley also had the dubious distinction of being the author of the 'Boo A Blue At Ballymore' slogan which was used to promote matches against New South Wales in Brisbane. He told me that he had made up his mind after that Scotland Test to unseat me if the opportunity arose, and he saw no reason to change his mind now. Then he made a curious remark. 'Actually, I quite like you as a bloke — I don't know why,' he said. I wasn't sure whether to feel flattered or not by this.

The vote was taken in late February, and Alan Jones won. I was at my desk at work when John Dedrick, the Australian Rugby Union's chief executive, phoned me with the news. I do not know for sure how the twelve votes were split, but from what I have been told unofficially I think there were probably five for Jones, five for me and two for Templeton. Because none of us had a clear majority, the issue was settled by preference votes. This is where the votes of the two Queensland delegates, Byrne and Crowley, were crucial. I believe both voted against me, and this determined the outcome. Thus, the selection of an Australian XV for a Test in 1982 may well have cost me the coaching job in 1984. The interesting thing is that the other two selectors who helped me choose that team were not required to pay the same price. Both were re-elected as selectors.

I told a journalist after I was deposed that I was terribly disappointed. In truth, I was heart-broken. It seemed to me that anyone with a thorough appreciation of the game would have recognised the special problems the team had been experiencing, not the least of them being the wholesale changes in personnel. Under the circumstances, I felt strongly that I deserved another term. If Bob Templeton had replaced me, it might not have been so hard to take. What I could not accept was that I deserved to be replaced by a coach with such limited experience as Jones. Evan Whitton of the *Sydney Morning Herald* wrote: 'To say that this decision is a disgrace will seem, to many supporters of the game, to elaborate the obvious."

It is one thing to be defeated. It is another to be defeated after having been subjected to a scurrilous campaign of denigration. I have been told by people who took part in the vote that they had been told very damaging things about me beforehand. It was far from a clean campaign. Stan Pilecki may have had this in mind when he said: 'They have stabbed him in the back.' I am sure Jones himself had nothing to do with the underhand campaign that was conducted against me personally. I know for a fact, though, that the people responsible were Jones supporters.

It seems some outrageous things were said about me in the weeks before the vote was taken. The most bizarre accusation of all, which was reported to me, was that I had disgraced the Australian Rugby Union by appearing at an official dinner after a Test in France with a 'tart' on each arm. The New Zealand Rugby writer Don Cameron heard this story, too. His response was that anyone capable of picking up two young women in France at one time deserved to be re-elected as coach because he must be a genius.

On a public level, various lines were peddled to the media. If a claim was made often enough and authoritively enough, it seemed, it became part of folklore and was universally accepted. It was said of me a number of times, for instance, that I was an 'inflexible' coach. I have no idea precisely what this meant because it was never explained. I do not know of any coach more flexible than me, according to my own definition of the word. I am totally flexible on the question of what the players do. All I am inflexible about is how they do it. On the other hand, it was said of Jones that he was a 'flexible' coach and, moreover, a superb selector. Ross Turnbull was quoted in the Sydney *Telegraph* describing Jones as possessing 'high flexibility'. I submit that Turnbull, like some of the other people who were saying things like this, had not the foggiest notion of what flexibility meant in terms of Rugby strategy. Perhaps they considered kicking the ball into the corners all day as being flexible.

It did not take long for the intense disappointment I felt after losing the job to fade. My resentment at the tactics used to undermine me has not faded even now. I do not remember ever being downcast to the point of wanting to give up coaching altogether. Within a few months, I think — certainly within a year — I had begun looking forward with certainty to the day that I got the job back.

11

THE JONES YEARS

Alan Jones put his imprint on the Australian team almost at once. He and his fellow selectors removed Mark Ella as captain and appointed Andrew Slack in his place. It is standard practice for the Australian coach's recommendation on the captaincy to weigh heavily with the other selectors, and I am sure the custom prevailed on this occasion. Two years earlier, in 1982, when Jones was manager of the New South Wales team, I happened to meet him at a restaurant in Sydney. We talked together for a few minutes, and during that time Jones spoke with enthusiasm of Ella's captaincy potential. Ella was, he said, a fine young man, wise beyond his years, a marvellous athlete, a splendid example for young Australians to follow, and so on. Mark Ella has told me that after we returned from the tour of France in late 1983 and it became clear Jones intended standing for the national coaching job, he took it upon himself, as Australian captain, to phone Jones and urge him to give up the idea. Ella told him he thought he was already doing a fine job as New South Wales manager and that he should continue in it. He said he also felt Bob Dwyer was doing well in his job and that the Australian team was headed in the right direction. In short, he was suggesting things be left as they were. This would hardly have endeared Mark Ella to the future Australian coach.

Jones had two great successes during his four years as coach, the grand slam victories in Britain and Ireland in 1984 and the series victory over New Zealand in 1986, which gave Australia the Bledisloe Cup. The team he took to Britain in 1984 was in all respects superior to the one I took to France a year earlier. In particular, it had been strengthened by the addition of Topo Rodriguez. As soon as Rodriguez joined the team, a good Australian scrum became a great one. Nick Farr-Jones made his first tour, too, although he was then obviously not the dominant figure on the field he was to become. The key to the whole enterprise, however, was undoubtedly Mark Ella. He played his natural game, and he played it very well. He was the orchestrator of the Australian victories.

Andrew Slack, who was immediately installed as Australian captain when Alan Jones took over as coach. Mike Brett

Jones made a number of intelligent decisions in 1984. He deserves credit, in my view, for bringing Steve Cutler on during the tour. We had taken Cutler to New Zealand in 1982 and, despite some opposition, we took him to France in 1983, where he suffered an injury and did not have the happiest of tours. I subsequently learned that Cutler felt very despondent about the France tour and was in need of reassurance and encouragement. I regret very much that I did not realise this myself. Jones did realise it, apparently, and under his influence Cutler blossomed on the tour in 1984.

David Codey's inclusion in the touring side was another good decision which, I assume, Jones had a lot to do with. I promoted Codey to the Test side straight from the New South Wales Country team in 1983, but he missed out on the tour of France later that year. Jones took him to Britain in 1984 and he made a big contribution there. I also think Jones made a wise and brave move when he positioned Michael Lynagh at inside-centre in place of Michael Hawker. By doing so he brought a good goal-kicker into the team while still leaving Ella at five-eighth to play his pivotal role.

Australia had three very successful years while Jones was coach, culminating in the Bledisloe Cup victory of 1986, when Australia defeated New Zealand by two Tests to one. We would have won the series three-nil but for an unbelievable refereeing decision in the second Test which denied Steve Tuynman a try. Tuynman went over the line with the ball beneath his body, but the referee refused to award a try because he could not see the ball. I was as astounded as Tuynman. Given the fact that a try-scorer is generally on top of the ball when he scores a try, I would have thought it fairly normal for the ball to be out of sight. If every referee took the same line, I think at least half the tries that have ever been scored would have been disallowed.

Defeating New Zealand was a fine achievement, even allowing for the fact that New Zealand was obviously below strength that year. The Cavaliers' tour of South Africa had thrown New Zealand Rugby into turmoil, and New Zealand went into the first Test with many untried players, having chosen deliberately to exclude the Cavaliers. Some of the Cavaliers were brought back for the second Test and more of them for the third Test. The Wallabies had a great victory in that third Test, withstanding one assault on the line after another, just as the Wallabies did in the World Cup final against England in 1991. I remember one tackle in particular by Topo Rodriguez. Close to the Australian line, he blocked Hika Reid, who was himself a powerful man, and then drove him backwards. That tackle certainly saved a try. Finally, when the New Zealanders had spent themselves, the Australians launched their own attack and ran out convincing winners.

I am not able to assess Jones' coaching skills. Only the players he coached are in a position to do that. I am experienced enough to realise that the type of coaching a team receives and the type of game it plays on

Nick Farr-Jones is hunted by Mark Shaw and Mike Brewer during the third test of the 1986 series at Eden Park. Australia won and returned home with the Bledisloe Cup.   Peter Bush

the field sometimes bear little resemblance to each other. What I do know is that the Australian team in 1984 played with more and more confidence as the tour went on, and the coach must be given credit for this. I admired some of the tactics Jones employed. He used his back-row forwards and scrum-half in attack very effectively, for instance. They moved the opposition defence one way and attacked the other way, a tactic I enjoy.

In one important area, mid-field play, there was a perceptible decline in the quality of the team's play during the Jones years. The obvious reason for this was the absence of Mark Ella after 1984. The worst thing that can be said about Jones's term as coach is that two outstanding players, Mark Ella and Steve Roche, chose to retire from the game prematurely rather than continue playing under him. I think Jones paid for this in the end, because as our mid-field play declined so did our capacity to score points.

This, I believe, was the primary cause of the team's disappointments in 1987.

Before a Test against Italy, Jones announced that he expected the team to score a point per minute. In my view, this was an unfortunate thing for him to say publicly, for we may be sure the Italian team felt insulted by it, and it was probably not a wise thing to say even privately, lest the players should go into the match expecting it to be easy. Australia did win the match, but not overwhelmingly, which indicated to me that here was a team not doing things accurately. When a first-division nation like Australia plays a second-division nation like Italy, it is the class of the Rugby it produces which determines the number of points it posts on the scoreboard. A few years before, when a United States side toured Australia, some of the teams it met thought they could win by simply overpowering the Americans. They thought they could just smash the Americans out of the way, but the Americans were good enough to cope with anything as basic as that. It is when the standard of play is raised one or two notches higher, when a team starts playing with speed and precision, that an ordinary opposition finds it difficult to cope.

It was a curious sensation for me in those years to watch the Australian team in action and not feel part of what was happening. On the other hand, I never lost the feeling of being personally involved, because most of the players out on the field had played in the teams I coached a year or more before. I was in the grandstand when Australia lost to France in the semi-final of the World Cup in 1987, and I felt devastated. I must have drooped physically in disappointment, because I remember my wife, Ruth, who was with me, asking if there was something the matter with me. After that, Australia lost to Wales in the play-off for third place at Rotorua. I considered this the poorest Australian performance I had seen in years. It seemed to me, viewing things from the outside, that the Australia players did not approach the match with a proper focus. Before the match Jones made it clear he saw no point in playing the match. Who cares which team comes third or fourth, he asked, and where is Rotorua anyway? This kind of talk could hardly have helped the team's mental preparation for the match.

After this Australia lost a series in Argentina. The fortunes of a team which had been soaring a year before had clearly gone into a dive. I watched the Argentina Tests on television, and it was clear to me that various things were not right. Australia was playing a game which was dependent on the individual skills of their mid-field players rather than on their collective skills. It is a common, if tragic, fact in Rugby that the sum of the players' individual skills rarely equals their collective capacity. There is no better example of this than the England team of 1991. England had three mid-field players who positively shone with individual brilliance — Rob Andrew, Will Carling and Jeremy Guscott — but collectively the

Mark Ella and Alan Jones with plenty to smile about after the Wallabies'
Grand Slam triumph in the UK in 1984.   John Fairfax Group

three made little impact on the Australian defence.

I can only assume that Jones had not concentrated on coaching collective mid-field play. Coaching it is not easy. It requires a thorough knowledge of the concept's intricacies plus an eye for the detail during the match so that adjustments can be made later. It is an area of the game on which I place great emphasis. Most good judges of Rugby who watched the World Cup matches in 1991 recognised Australia's immense capability in this area and, moreover, recognise it as being unique.

Many people, wanting to be nice, have expressed the view to me that the Australian team would have been just as successful, and possibly more successful, in the mid-1980s if I had been the coach instead of Alan Jones. My reply has always been, 'Maybe I would have done it. But Jones *did* it.' Nobody can take that away from him.

12

BACK IN BUSINESS

Alan Jones came up for re-election in February 1988 and I stood against him. I knew it would not be an easy contest to win. Ross Turnbull was still a powerful influence in New South Wales Rugby affairs, and it was clear Jones had the support of the New South Wales delegates, who controlled five of the twelve votes. On the other hand, I was aware there was a campaign under way to unseat Jones and that several players were behind it. A few of them approached me and suggested I should stand. I told them I already intended doing so. They suggested then that I should set out to lobby the people who would be voting on the appointment. I declined. For one thing, it would be a messy, time-consuming exercise. For another, I didn't want to put myself in the position of having to promote myself as a better coach than Jones and beg for votes. That would have been belittling.

I won the ballot, but only narrowly. The press speculated that the vote was split seven-five or six-six, and from my own sources I gathered it was as close as this. A six-six split was a possibility. Ordinarily, the chairman would have voted for Jones' retention in the event of a six-six vote, but I think the prevailing attitude within the Australian Rugby Union executive was such that a six-six vote may well have resulted in Jones' defeat. The upshot was that I displaced Jones from the position which he had displaced me from four years before. In 1988, as in 1984, no words of commiseration or congratulation were exchanged between us.

A few days after the vote, Jones was reported by the Sydney *Sun* newspaper to have named David Campese on radio as being 'one of the architects' of his defeat. According to the *Sun*, Jones believed Campese had undermined his position by making phone calls to influential people. I have no first-hand knowledge of what happened, yet I find it hard to believe that Campese could have played any serious role in the move against Jones. It is simply not Campese's style to campaign on an issue of this kind. There were some other players who did campaign, however, and

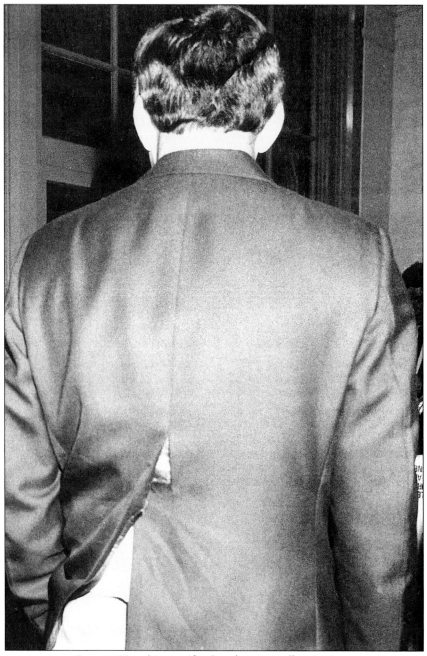

Came 1988 and it was Alan Jones' turn to suffer rejection.

Col Whelan

a few of them have never tried to conceal the fact. There was nothing personal in this. I happen to know that the players who were most active in the campaign against Jones were also quick to defend Jones' contribution to Australian Rugby. They thought Jones had done a fine job for two or three years, but they felt a need for a change now because it seemed to them that the wheels were falling off the wagon.

I admired the extent of the loyalty which the players felt towards Alan Jones. My impression was that all the players felt some loyalty to him and some felt a strong loyalty to him. With this in mind, and realising that the transfer of control from Jones to myself would not be easy for everyone, I invited three of the players, Nick Farr-Jones, Simon Poidevin and Steve Cutler, to dinner at my home. These three were not only senior members of the team but were, I thought, players who felt they owed loyalty to Jones. There were just the four of us at the table and the atmosphere was relaxed. I told them that if they felt a personal attachment to Jones that was fine with me. Given that he had coached them for four years, I thought it was desirable that they should.

On the other hand, I said the fact had to be recognised that Jones was now a member of the media — he was an announcer on the Sydney radio station 2UE — and, moreover, he might well be antagonistic towards the present team administration. Under these circumstances, I suggested to the three players that in conversations with Jones they should be careful when discussing team affairs. It was one thing to discuss team affairs with friends. It was another to discuss them with a friend if there was a chance that some adverse comment might rebound in public on the team.

A few months later I said much the same thing to Brian Smith, who was known to be friendly with Jones. It occurred to me that Smith might think his friendship with Jones would somehow count against him now that I was coach. I assured him this was not the case, that it did not make the slightest difference to me who his friends were, but I also urged him to be careful when discussing team affairs with Jones, given that Jones worked in the media. If he was unhappy with my coaching methods or our tactics, for instance, it would be unwise of him to pass on his criticism to Jones. By suggesting this, I was not reflecting badly on Jones. As a broadcaster dealing with public issues, he would simply have been doing his job to raise such a matter on the air.

Unfortunately, I think Brian Smith was not prepared to accept my assurance on this. He gave me the impression that he felt his relationship with Jones did influence my attitude towards him and, therefore, affected his prospects of playing for Australia. He was chosen as a reserve for the Tests that year, but I think he was unhappy at not being chosen in the fifteen. At the start of the season he played for Australia against a World XV in place of Michael Lynagh who was injured, and he played well and scored a lot of points. He may have felt on the strength of that performance

*Brian Smith . . . a skilful player who abandoned rugby to play for Alan Jones'
league team Balmain.*   Mike Brett

that he deserved a place in the fifteen. I know Alan Jones thought so. He made this plain enough on radio. Michael Lynagh's position in the team was not earned in a day, and nor should it have been lost in a day. In any case, although Smith played extremely well as an individual in that match against the World XV, I saw little evidence of his being able to play a team-oriented game from the five-eighth position. I thought he had the potential to become a valuable Test player one day, but it was likely to be in some other position which allowed him to play as an individual.

We selected Smith as a reserve, but it seemed he was unhappy with this. As a result, some tensions arose which affected Michael Lynagh adversely, and I tried to deal with the situation by having a meeting with the two players, Smith and Lynagh. Subsequently, Smith left for Oxford. The next thing we heard was that he was turning out for Ireland. After that, he returned to Australia to play Rugby League for Alan Jones' team, Balmain. If Smith had not left, I think there is every chance he would have played for Australia by now. He was a reserve, after all, which meant he was knocking on the door of the team. He was big, fast and strong, and he possessed good kicking skills and good running skills. Fullback and outside-centre are two positions he might have suited, although it is unlikely now we will ever know this for sure.

To be back in business in my old position was immensely satisfying for me. I did not feel I was taking on a burden. On the contrary, I felt as if a huge load had been lifted off my shoulders. I felt free again. After my reappointment I spent time in deep and honest reflection. I was conscious of the need not to make too many changes too quickly, and I was also conscious of the need to keep in place all that had been positive and successful in the team during the time Jones had coached it. In the four years since I last coached the team it had become stronger in some respects and weaker in others. The front row in 1987 was certainly more effective than in 1983. Not only was Topo Rodriguez there, but Tommy Lawton and Andy McIntyre were four years older, stronger and more capable. The team's lineout-winning ability was also greater in 1987 than in 1983. On the other hand, the integrated mid-field play in 1987 was inferior to the mid-field play in 1983.

By 1988, these comparisons had ceased to be relevant, since the departure of so many players had fundamentally changed the composition of the side. At the end of 1987 quite a few senior players had chosen to retire or move to Rugby League. These players had apparently been delaying their departure so they could play in the World Cup, but as soon as the World Cup was over there was an exodus of them. Topo Rodriguez and Andy McIntyre, the mainstays of the Australian scrum, retired. Two of our most experienced backs, Roger Gould and Andrew Slack, retired and two of our most talented backs, Brett Papworth and Matt Burke, went to League. Troy Coker and, later, Brian Smith went to Oxford. In my first year as coach, 1982, ten leading players had made themselves unavailable to play for Australia. In 1988, my first year back, I found myself presented with a similar problem.

The retirements and defections to League continued into 1988. James Grant and Andrew Leeds were two others who moved to League. The problem was compounded by the fact that a number of players, including Simon Poidevin and Steve Cutler, were reluctant to tour. I calculated later that in a fifteen-month period starting in late 1987 we lost thirteen players who had either made it to the international level or appeared on the verge of making it, and unfortunately a high proportion of these were mid-field players. The extent of these changes in personnel was particularly evident at the 1991 World Cup. Only five of the Australians who played in that tournament had played in the World Cup matches four years before. They were Nick Farr-Jones, Simon Poidevin, David Campese, Michael Lynagh and Troy Coker.

A few days after my reappointment as coach, the Sydney *Sun* quoted me as saying, 'You can't change things too quickly, otherwise people become nervous and uncertain.' I moved too hastily in certain directions when I first took on the job in 1982, and I was alert to the danger of making the same mistake again. I was more than happy to preserve a number of Alan Jones' ideas. When Farr-Jones, Poidevin and Cutler had dinner at my home, I said to them there were sure to be a number of things in Jones' method of team preparation and in his tactical approach which had proved successful and which therefore should be retained. I told them that I was strongly in favour of team members speaking up when necessary and saying, 'Jonesy used to do it this way, and we think it's not a bad idea and that we ought to consider it.' I told them I might not necessarily agree with the idea, but that I would always welcome the opportunity to discuss it.

Jones employed a tactic of trying to force opposing teams under pressure into the corners of the field, from which they would often have trouble escaping. I thought this was one of his best strategies. It was not Jones' invention, of course, but it was a strategy he operated very successfully by making use of Michael Lynagh's kicking skills in particular. It proved to be of great advantage in Australia's match against Ireland in the 1987 World Cup. It was the key to a tremendous Australian onslaught in the first thirty minutes of that match Previously, I had not chosen to use this tactic myself. It was not that I disagreed with it in principle; I have already made the point that there is nothing wrong with kicking to move defences around. I was simply preoccupied with other methods of attack. Since Jones' departure in 1988, however, it has remained part of the Australian armoury. When I see a need for it I simply have to say to Lynagh, 'Noddy, just put a few kicks down there like you did against Ireland in '87.'

On the other hand, there were some practices established or at least

Alan Jones . . . we were poles apart philosophically as coaches.   Mike Brett

permitted by Jones which I dispensed with at once. One of these was the creation of an elite group within the team. This wasn't something I stumbled upon when I became coach again. The existence of such an elite group was generally recognised within the Rugby community while Jones was the coach. It was widely believed, for instance, that certain players were told before the Test team was selected that they would be playing. Jones may well have encouraged the formation of the elite group, believing that it would lift performances. He and I were poles apart philosophically on this point. As I understand it, Jones believed that if you aspire to elitism you will automatically aim higher and perform better. This may work in the short term. Maybe it does give the players a psychological burst which carries them through a match or two. Over the long term, however, I have no doubt that it harms a team's performance. It was, I believe, a major cause of dissatisfaction among the players during the Jones years.

There was another legacy of the Jones years which I saw a need to deal with. I refer to the souring of relations with certain other Rugby nations which had occurred while he was coach. Jones said openly that he did not see it as his role as Australian coach to go around the world making a popular fellow of himself. On overseas tours he rubbed many people up the wrong way. His motives, no doubt, were honourable. I think his aim was to foster a tough, combative attitude among the players, and one way to do this was to adopt a tough, combative attitude himself. He was prepared to wear the unpopularity that this attracted to him. Unfortunately, unpopularity was also attracted to the team. In the international Rugby community, Australian players ceased to be regarded as 'good blokes'. I know it is Jones' view that other countries regard you as good blokes only if they beat you, but this is not true, as I know from my own experience. Since becoming coach again, a few of the players and I have made a special effort to rebuild bridges between Australia and the rest of the Rugby world which took a battering in the Jones years.

I have heard people speak of a feud between myself and Alan Jones. The term 'feud' suggests an active hostility. In fact, I cannot remember Jones and I ever exchanging a single unpleasant word. From time to time he has criticised me on his radio program, sometimes quite harshly. If I had worked as a radio announcer, perhaps I would have criticised him. There has been no feud as such between us. There has been an apparent mutual antagonism, certainly, but it has been passive. We are so different in personality that I do not believe we could ever have found a common wave length.

Towards the end of 1990 the Variety Club held a luncheon to honour Jones for the fund-raising work he had done on its behalf. I had helped the Variety Club in a small way myself, so I appreciated the fine effort Jones had made and decided to attend the lunch. I think he was surprised to see me there, but he came up to say hello and shake hands, although I think he did it with a little embarrassment. Seeing an opportunity, a television crew trained their camera on us, and in the spirit of the moment Jones said, 'Get a close-up, boys. Bob Dwyer and Alan Jones shaking hands — that's not a sight you'll see too often.' Also in the spirit of the moment, I told the camera crew that Alan was congratulating me on our success in the third Test against the All Blacks. I resented the tactics his supporters used to depose me in 1984, but I have no hard feelings against him. I respect him for many of his achievements. I hope he respects me for some of mine.

13

COACHING –
AN HONOURABLE PROFESSION

Rugby is a complex game as games go, yet it is only a game. To coach it successfully you don't need to have the intellect of a nuclear physicist. What you need is some experience, a lot of common sense and a touch of imagination. There is one other requirement — a good memory.

Some time ago I sat next to Ken Catchpole at a Rugby dinner and, as usual, we ended the evening debating various Rugby matters over a bottle of port. On this evening Catchpole challenged me to explain how it was possible for one person to coach a whole team, since the coach could not possibly know everything there was to know about every position. I replied that I knew some things about all positions and a lot of things about some positions. I added that I never forgot anything useful I was told about any position. Catchpole questioned whether my memory was capable of this, so I repeated to him things he himself had told me when we played together for Randwick more than twenty-five years before. One was that after you pass the ball your hands should not travel in an arc so they are pointing somewhere behind you but, rather, should remain pointing towards the receiver. Another was that after charging down a kick you should never look for the ball but just keep running, the reason being that if the ball goes towards the opposition try-line you will be able to take advantage of it and if it doesn't go towards the try-line you would not have been able to take advantage of it, anyway.

Catchpole agreed, with apparent surprise, that he had indeed told me these things all those years before. At the time I thought they made sense, so I remembered them, and for years now I have been passing them on to players I have coached. As I went on to point out to Catchpole that same evening, he was by no means the only person who had taught me things about Rugby. Peter Johnson, a long-serving Australian hooker, told me long ago that when a hooker strikes for the ball he should not try to sweep it but, rather, he should strike at it like a snake and pull his toes right back, since the angle of his foot on the ball gave the angle of deflection. This seemed logical to me, and I have never forgotten it. I suppose I have a thousand pieces of information like this in my head. At least five hundred were put there by Cyril Towers alone. Accumulating information in this way is, I believe, an essential part of a coach's education. A coach cannot remember everything he hears. What he has to do is assess what he hears and then remember what is useful.

A wise coach has to keep learning, and he has to keep developing and varying his tactics, if only to prevent the opposition knowing what to expect. Other variations in tactics are forced on you by the type of players available. The World Cup team in 1991 did not play the same as the Australian team I coached in 1982, because the 1991 team was a different type of team. It had a much stronger forward pack, for example.

I am pleased to say I do not over-estimate the value of a coach's contribution to a team's performance. If there are fifteen players on the field and one coach on the sideline, then I consider the coach's input to be about one sixteenth of the total, or about 7 per cent. This isn't false modesty. I genuinely believe that this is about the extent of a coach's influence on a top-level team's performances. At the same time, I do think that a contribution of this size can have a critical bearing on how a team performs. I long ago read something about coaching which, with the benefit of experience, I have come to regard as true. It is that a coach cannot win without good athletes, but he can certainly lose with them. Each year, the Rugby League competition in Sydney provides examples of this — teams with good players which keep losing.

As coach, the quality I have valued most highly in my players is reliability of performance. This is something I have often told the players in the Australian team. In other words, the most valuable service a player can give his coach is not occasionally brilliant play but predictably good play. It could even be argued from a coach's standpoint that it doesn't matter too much how well a player performs so long as he performs as well as the coach expects him to. The unpredictable player, the player you cannot count on to do this or that, is a headache for the coach because you cannot confidently made him a part of a combination, and Rugby is a combination game. The wheel turns best when each cog is doing what is expected of it.

One of my firmest beliefs as a coach, which I constantly impress upon my players, is that they need to be task-focused, not goal-focused. By that I mean they should ignore the scoreboard entirely, for the figures posted on the scoreboard cannot influence what happens on the field. The things that enable you to score points when the score is nil-all are exactly the same things that enable you to score points when the score is 20-nil or nil-20. All any team needs to focus on is the task at hand. I have advocated this for as long as I have coached Rugby. It is a notion I developed myself,

A wise coach has to keep learning and he has to keep developing and varying his tactics. Do I look wise enough?

John Fairfax Group

and I have never heard anyone suggest the same thing until shortly before the 1991 World Cup when I read an article written by David Kirk, the All Blacks' captain at the 1987 World Cup. Kirk said in the article that scoring points and winning games was not a function in itself but simply a by-product of playing well. Although he expressed it in a slightly different way, this was precisely the point I had been making for years. Kirk went on to add, to my considerable satisfaction, that he thought the Australian players recognised this and that this was why he thought they would win the 1991 World Cup.

I cannot cite a better example of a player being task-focused than Michael Lynagh in the last few minutes of the 1991 World Cup match against Ireland. The situation, remember, was that Ireland took the lead close to full time, and Lynagh, the captain, had to marshal the team for a last-minutes effort. It would have been useless for him to berate the players, as some captains might have done in a similar situation, saying: 'We've got to score, we've got to score.' Lynagh did not do this. Instead, he said something like: 'Look, this is what we're going to do. I'm going to get the ball up there, you make sure you put them under pressure so we have the best chance of keeping them down there, and when we get down there you blokes win the ball and we'll score a try.' This is what they did, and he was the one who scored it.

Coaches must be prepared to use whatever resources are available, even if it means going outside Rugby. I have sometimes made use of Rugby League players, for instance. After regaining the national coaching job in 1988, I began placing a lot of emphasis on defence and introduced new tackling drills for the team. In February 1991 I invited one of Rugby League's most feared tacklers, Terry Randall, to come and speak to the players. At first, Randall seemed reserved and uncomfortable. Players were asking him questions about defence techniques and he was providing minimal answers. After we had all been pussy-footing like this for some time, Tim Gavin asked him how he managed to get so much shoulder drive into the tackle. If he was tackling with his right shoulder, Gavin asked, did he try to get his right leg driving in behind the shoulder, or what? The question brought Randall out of his shell. 'I don't know about any of that crap,' he said. 'I just want to kill the bastard.' The spell was broken, and from then on Randall was a font of information. We went on to the field for practical demonstrations, and although he had been out of the game for some years Randall joined in. It was a hot, dry, dusty day in February, but everyone threw himself into it, especially Randall, who tackled with a ferocity which, I think, was an eye-opener to some of our players. By the end the session, everyone was covered with the grime of dust mixed with perspiration yet more than satisfied with what had been a productive effort.

I am sorry to say that few, if any, coaches at the state and grade levels in Australia seem prepared to devote attention to fundamental principles of technique. This does not make the job of national coach any easier. I have found it hard work getting certain backline players in the Australian team even to do something as basic as reaching for the ball and passing it across their body. Frankly, there are some players in the present Australian team who have poor passing techniques. When they pass the ball you can never be sure where it will end up. One of them, a left-hander, is a poor passer to his left. With this in mind, I warned one of his team-mates at training one day, 'Don't call that move going left, because anything could happen,' but the team-mate brushed this aside, saying that everything would be all right. So they tried the move at training that day, and the pass did go astray, as I warned it might. The player I spoke to came up to me afterwards and said, 'You were right — he does have a problem on his left.' He had played alongside this player for years and not recognised it before.

The Australian team of 1991 was a great side, but it has the potential to be greater. Its tremendous potential was never fully realised because quite a few of the players had not developed their basic and collective skills to a standard which matched their athletic ability. There was little I could do about this. Before home matches, the national coach is allowed only three days with the team. This is a stupid ruling, incidentally, which is sure to be changed one day, but in the meantime we in Australia continue to adhere to it. In Britain, they effectively ignore it. There, coaches get together regularly with their national squads at weekends. They are allowed to do this because strictly the law applies only to the national *team*, not to the national squad. We in Australia would like to get around the ruling in the same way, but the cost of flying a squad together in Australia would be prohibitive, given the vast distances many players would have to travel.

Probably the most common fault of coaches is that they are not demanding enough. I remember saying to my assistant coaches at Randwick some years ago that we weren't running a child-minding service — mothers weren't sending their sons along to us so we could look after them two nights a week from 6.30 pm to 8.30 pm. It was our responsibility to help these players become better players between 6.30 pm and 8.30 pm. It is no use just going through the motions. The coach has to be attentive to detail. He must make sure the players do things exactly right. Practice does not make perfect. Only perfect practice makes perfect. If you practise doing something in an imperfect way, you end up being very good at doing it imperfectly. The measure of a coach's success is not whether the team wins or loses. It is whether his players were better players at the end of the season than they were at the start.

Coaching is fun and it can provide enormous satisfaction. In the year that I first coached Australia, I also coached Randwick sixths as a way of keeping my hand in. I loved it. I had them doing scissors passes and other backline moves. I used to roar at them at training for being out of position and making other mistakes, but they didn't mind that. They weren't turning up at training to fill in time, either. I have on my mantlepiece at home a beer mug with 'Sixth-Grade Coach' engraved on it. I treasure it as a memory of a happy, satisfying experience.

I take pride in the fact that my teams have always had a reputation for playing a fifteen-man game. It usually comes as a surprise to people, therefore, that we hardly ever train as a fifteen-man unit. Before a home Test we generally have about six hours of practice. On average, I doubt whether the team would spend more than twenty minutes of this time training as a team. More often than not, the only reason I have them training as a team even for twenty minutes is that the players have requested it. Sometimes I split the team into groups of seven and eight. Sometimes the split is five and ten. Occasionally, I have them split in three groups of five. My reasoning here is that no Rugby match is a single entity. It is merely a collection of individual incidents, and what we need to do at training is practice the things we do in all those individual incidents.

It is true that in some movements all fifteen players are involved, but it is not necessary for them to practise these movements as a fifteen. Instead, I will say to one group at training, 'If you blokes practise your part of it correctly, the other group will know what you're doing because I'll tell them, and I'll tell get them to practise how they can capitalise on it. So you fellas just concentrate on doing your part of it correctly, and leave the rest to me.' In this way, it is possible for a coach to have the whole team working together like clockwork in a match without having to waste time training them together. A Rugby match is rather like a Meccano set in this way. The individual pieces are separate when you buy the set, but because they are designed to fit together you can build something out of them. What the Rugby coach has to do with his team is make sure all the pieces are correctly manufactured so that they fit together.

In the late 1980s, when I was doing a coaching tour through British Columbia in Canada, I watched an up-country team called Fraser Valley get trounced by a huge number of points. Its backs stood as deep as I have ever seen a backline stand, and time after time they were knocked over fifteen or twenty metres behind the advantage line. Yet I thought the team had some good players. In fact, one of them was Gordie MacKinnon, the widely acclaimed World Cup open-side flanker who played for the World XV against New Zealand in New Zealand's centenary celebrations in 1992. McKinnon had already come to my notice as a player of unusual ability. I had examined a written report on various fitness assessments which had been done on the Canadian players, and I noticed that MacKinnon's statistics were impressive. It was obvious MacKinnon was an outstanding athlete, so I inquired about him. My Canadian informant told me that he was a flanker and proceeded to give me a brief description of his talents and skills. Then he added: 'There's one other thing worth mentioning about him — he hunts grizzly bears for a hobby.' It seemed to me then that he must be a useful man on the field.

So I joined the Fraser Valley players at their next training session. I began by saying that I had watched them play, that I thought their play was terrible and that they would have no hope of winning if they kept playing that way. I then suggested that their backline should stand flatter. They rejected this at once, saying that they had good wingers and that they wanted to make sure of getting the ball out to them by standing deep. I asked them to show me how they normally did this, which they did. Using witch's hats, I marked the position of the half-back when he passed the ball and the position of the winger when he finally received it.

Having done this, I got them them to practise passing the ball for fifteen minutes or so. I told them to reach for the ball and transfer it smoothly to the other side. Then I got them to repeat the exercise of passing the ball out to the winger, this time lining up flat as I had suggested. I told them I did not care how long any of them took to pass the ball, so long as he did not bring the ball into his body as he did so. The half-back positioned himself at the witch's hat where he had been before, and out the ball went. To the amazement of the players, when the ball reached the winger he was actually further from the imaginary defence than he had been before, despite the fact that he had started out much closer. A simple lesson in technique had transformed the speed of transmission of the ball. So we practised lining up flat. I told the centres to attack the defence, to hang on to the ball if they did not feel they could pass it, but to make sure they did not lose the ball when they were tackled.

The next weekend they played Vancouver Island, the competition leader, and they thrashed them. It was probably the first time Vancouver Island's defence had ever been threatened. There is nothing unusual about this. How many teams are there in the Sydney competition, I wonder, which have never found out whether the opposition could defend, for the simple reason they never threatened their defence? This can never be said about New Zealand. A team always knows whether it can tackle or not after it plays New Zealand.

I have often found that you can get players to accept your logic by showing them the absurdity of the alternative. Once, when I was coaching a boys' team at St Patrick's College at Strathfield in Sydney, a winger told me he did not agree with the flat backline formation I was suggesting because he feared the centres would always be tackled before they could get the ball to him. I asked him why he wanted the ball anyway, and he replied that he had good pace and wanted to run around the defence and score a try. I said that sounded reasonable to me, so I proposed an experiment. I got the backline to line up in a row directly behind the halfback, which in practice meant that each player virtually had to throw the ball over his shoulder to pass it to the next. It was plainly ludicrous and the boys laughed, but I said to the winger, 'Believe me, I am not trying to make fun of you. I am just showing how I can make certain you do get the ball. If you line up like this, you are *guaranteed* to get the ball every time — the defence will be nowhere near enough to stop it. So what do think of it?' The winger thought the formation was stupid. When I asked him to specify why, he said it was stupid to stand right back there when you wanted to score a try right up there. I said to him this was precisely the point I was making in the first place.

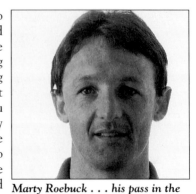

Marty Roebuck . . . his pass in the World Cup final provided me with a moment of deep satisfaction.

I think I am probably unlike most coaches in being a stickler for detail. It is by attending to the fine details of the game that I actually derive my greatest satisfaction from coaching. I have described elsewhere how I hammered home the message to the players that in passing they should reach for the ball and then swing it across their bodies. One of the most exciting moments for me in the World Cup final in 1991 was when Marty Roebuck reached for a pass under pressure and swung the ball across his body to Campese, who broke away and kicked ahead. If the ball had not taken an eccentric bounce and hit the referee, who was therefore obliged to set a scrum, this would certainly have resulted in a try. Although it did not lead to a try, Roebuck's pass provided me with a moment of deep satisfaction, because we had practised it hundreds of times.

Especially in the type of backline play that I teach, detail is everything. At the end of the World Cup final in 1991, I made a mental note to take Tim Horan and Jason Little aside at the start of the following season and get them to watch a video of two occasions in the match when, by running at a slight angle instead of straight, they possibly cost us a try.

People have sometimes asked me how I can stand the pressure of being coach of a national team. I have found it hard to explain to them that it is actually the pressure of the job which attracts me. I believe most coaches (and maybe most players, too) are hooked on the emotional charge which it provides — the fears, the great expectations, the thrills, the surprises and even the bitter disappointments. Perhaps they are simply addicted to the adrenalin which these emotions generate. I don't think I have gone through one season as coach without giving serious thought to retiring. 'I've had enough,' I think to myself. 'I'll resign at the end of the season.' Within two weeks of the season ending, however, I experience withdrawal symptoms. I know then I would miss coaching too much to do without it.

A PROMISE OF GREATER THINGS

By 1989, I was being criticised increasingly over the erratic form of the Australian team. Our performances since I resumed coaching the team in the previous year had tended to be either highs or lows, and I was aware that people were seeing a similarity between this and my record in 1982 and 1983. 'Here we go again,' some of them were saying. I did not welcome the criticism, of course, but I was not overly concerned about the team's chequered performance. I knew enough about Rugby to realise that inconsistency is nearly always a sign that a team has potential but is still developing. A team like this can produce a superb performance on its day provided everything goes right. If things start to go wrong, it does not have the depth of confidence and concentration, which go hand in hand, to pull through. This was the story of the Australian team in 1988 and 1989.

In 1988 we drew with an exceptionally powerful All Blacks side in Brisbane, the only Test the All Blacks failed to win in four years from 1987 to 1990. It was an outstanding performance by what was really a makeshift team, yet in that same series against New Zealand we suffered two heavy defeats. Similarly, we were defeated by England on our tour of Britain later that year, yet won impressively against Scotland. In 1989, we won well against the Lions in the first Test, then lost the next two Tests against them, one by a single point. To some observers of the game, this seemed to indicate a disturbing pattern.

All this while I had been adhering to my policy of not making too many changes too quickly. Half-way through the 1989 season, however, after we had been beaten by the Lions, I told my two co-selectors, John Bain and Bob Templeton, that I felt the time had come to make some bold decisions. I argued that the team was not progressing fast enough nor in the right direction. Abrupt changes were needed, and we had to make them now if we wanted to become the top side in the world. Some of the decisions might be risky, I said, but if we were smart we could minimise the risk.

*Lloyd Walker scoring Australia's only try in the third test against the 1988
All Blacks in Sydney.*   *Peter Bush*

I tabled a list of players I thought should be dropped and a list of players
who I thought could take their place. The names on the second list were
by no means obvious contenders for the team. I suggested Phil Kearns,
then Randwick's reserve-grade hooker and hooker for the New South
Wales B team. I considered him a player of the future and urged that he
should go straight into the Test against the All Blacks the following week.
I suggested Tony Daly as loose-head prop. He looked the part. He was
strong, fit and mobile, as loose-heads ought to be. He had no experience
at all in senior representative Rugby, but he had played in the Australian
under-21 team and the information I had managed to collect about him
— from the experienced coach Alec Evans, among others — confirmed
my view that he had the capacity to succeed at the top level. I suggested
he should make his debut in representative Rugby by marking Richard Loe
at Eden Park, Auckland, a few days later.

I had another front-rower on my list, Ewen McKenzie. He was injured,
so he could not be considered for the coming Test, but I suggested he
should be marked down as future tight-head prop. I suggested Tim Horan.
Although he was only eighteen years old and had not advanced beyond
the Queensland B team, I thought he was capable of making the big step
up to Test Rugby, and I suggested we play him at once as outside-centre.

Finally, there was Simon Poidevin. He had announced he was not available for representative Rugby, but I thought he might come back if prevailed upon. I suggested we prevail upon him at once.

All these players took the field against New Zealand a week later and performed well, even if the team did not win. There was a tour of France coming up later in the year, and it seemed to me that this offered us an ideal opportunity to press ahead with rebuilding the team. Ewen McKenzie went into the touring side from New South Wales B; Brendan Nasser went in from Queensland B; Tim Gavin went in from New South Wales B; Jason Little, eighteen years old, went in from Queensland B. The thirty players who went on the tour of France provided us with a very good first XV and six or seven good reserves. Thereafter the standard tailed off, one reason being that quite a few leading players, such as Simon Poidevin, Jeff Miller and Steve Cutler, were not available to tour.

We began in promising fashion. We won in fine style against Cote Basque at Toulouse and Cote D'Azur at Toulon, and after this match Nick Farr-Jones declared that he had never known an Australian team to play a better half of Rugby than this team did in the first half of the match. Even

Ewen McKenzie and Tony Daly, two of the exciting new players introduced to the Wallabies in 1989. Photosport

if Farr-Jones was over-stating things in the excitement of the moment, it was a most encouraging observation. In the first Test at Strasbourg, we inflicted on France the heaviest defeat it had ever sustained on French soil. The score was 32 to 15. The French were astounded that a team containing so many little-known, inexperienced players could have done this to them. It was Jason Little's first Test, Tim Horan's second and Phil Kearns' second. Altogether, seven of the Australian XV were playing either their first or second Test.

France won the second Test by 25 to 19, squaring the series. I returned home to Australia in November 1989 to learn that Alan Jones had just said on his radio program that my record as coach was 'abysmal' and that I should be dumped. I did not know why Jones was so critical of me and so eager for me to be replaced as national coach, although I did wonder later if perhaps he was seeking to advance the cause of his old friend and co-coach Alec Evans, who was a candidate for the job.

Michael Lynagh was asked about Jones' comment and replied, 'Bob had a tough job and I feel he did very well on tour. With the team he had, with the young players and the more mature ones, Dwyer gathered us all around and we were a very tight-knit unit.' My own comment, quoted in the press next day, was, 'There is no one in France who doesn't think Australia is a major threat in the 1991 World Cup.' This was entirely accurate. Although we lost one of the Tests and four of the provincial games, the French were deeply impressed by the type of Rugby the team played. The French coach Jacques Fouroux went so far as to nominate Australia as favourite to win the World Cup two years later. Clearly, this Frenchman could see a potential in the Australian team which Jones, an Australian, could not.

In 1990, France came to Australia to play us in a three-Test series. We toughed it out for a win in the first Test, won the second in an exceptionally open, high-scoring encounter, and lost the third. This single loss dampened some people's spirits, but I was convinced now that we were heading in the right direction. After that, we went to New Zealand minus several key players. Our three leading open-side flankers, Simon Poidevin, Jeff Miller and David Wilson, were all unavailable to tour. On top of that Brendan Nasser, whom we were looking at to fill the vacancy, was injured and missed the first Test. Jason Little had to pull out of the tour, too, because of an injury. It was a tough tour, but our level of performance rose steadily and peaked in the final Test in Wellington, which we won convincingly, 21 to 6. It was the first Test New Zealand had lost since 1986. That win convinced me and, I believe, also convinced the players that the various measures we had taken to lift our performance, including, in particular, the introduction of a scientifically based physical preparation program, were paying off. Unmistakably, we could detect in the air the promise of greater things.

15

ALL IN THE PREPARATION

I could not count the number of times I have been asked to reveal the secret of Australia's victory in the 1991 World Cup. It is widely assumed some kind of 'secret' must exist — that to win the tournament we must have hit upon something nobody else thought of. In fact, we did hit upon something. It was not on the Rugby field but in the sports laboratory. The secret to our success, if there was one, was the scientifically based program of physical preparation which we began implementing among Australia's elite players in late 1989. More than anything else, I believe, this made the difference between ourselves and the rest of the world at the World Cup two years later.

I had recognised the lack of a proper preparation program in Australian Rugby quite a few years before, and as far back as the mid-1980s I had developed a program to try to fill the gap at the Randwick club. The New Zealanders had woken up to the need for it about the same time and had already instituted a scheme of their own. After regaining the national coaching job in 1988, I set about trying to develop a program for the Australian team. By the end of the year we had a well-researched scheme in operation which began to produce results from 1990 onwards. It was comprehensive, covering areas such as strength, fitness, diet and sports psychology. Implementing it was not an easy undertaking. Apart from anything else, it required Australian Rugby players to undergo a kind of cultural transformation.

These were not the first steps which Rugby took in this direction, of course. In the late 1970s there was a resurgence of Australian Rugby after three fairly lean decades. True, Australia enjoyed a purple patch in the 1960s when a number of talented players — Ken Catchpole, John Thornett, Rob Hemming and others — happened to come to the fore together. For much of the fifties and seventies, however, Australian Rugby was in a slump. The upturn in the late seventies was, in my opinion, a direct result of a decision by the Australian Rugby Union to improve the way the team was prepared. The ARU took stock of itself and decided something had to be done to make the Australian team more competitive. For the sake of the game in Australia, it could not afford to have the national team go on losing as it had been. As a first step, the ARU appointed a national director of coaching, a move which followed a visit to Australia by the national director of coaching in Wales, Ray Williams. Some people would argue that Australia's recent success can ultimately be traced to this single event. Indeed, I have heard the president of the ARU, Joe French, say more than once that Australia has Wales to thank for rescuing it from the doldrums in the seventies

By comparison with other international sports such as athletics and swimming and even with certain football codes such as American Football and Rugby League in Australia, Rugby Union always provided its players with a fairly primitive form of physical preparation. I do not know why this was so. Perhaps it is because Rugby was an amateur sport and its administrators shied away instinctively from the type of intensive programs associated with professional sportspeople. However that may be, it happened that in 1988, about the time I was trying to do something about this deficiency, Rugby was added to the list of sports covered by the government-funded Australian Institute of Sport in Canberra. Two Rugby coaches were appointed to the staff there, David Clark as head coach and Brian O'Shea as senior coach. These two men were able to draw on the expertise of all the institute's specialists — physiologists, biomechanists, nutritionists and so on. They and I discussed various ideas, as a result of which an outline of a program began to emerge.

I looked everywhere for the right person to run the program. I wanted someone who had a sound academic base, but I also wanted someone who was successful in a practical sense, too. We looked as far afield as Canada, the United States and Britain. Finally, I was convinced by a couple of experts we consulted in the United States that the very best person for the job was right on our doorstep, an Australian living in Australia. He was Dr Frank Pyke, who had first made a name for himself in the 1970s by guiding the recovery of the celebrated Australian cricketer Dennis Lillee from a serious back injury.

Pyke said he would be happy to help, so I arranged for him to attend a meeting with myself, Clark, O'Shea and the Rothmans national director of coaching, Dick Marks. At this meeting we decided on a course of action. We appointed experts in various fields around Australia to help us design the program we needed. We called upon fitness consultants, strength consultants, dieticians and sports psychologists. A program gradually started to take shape — too gradually for my liking. I found myself impatient to see the concept ready to go into operation, but I was advised on all sides that what we were doing was simply too important to be rushed. Finally, in the winter of 1989, we were ready to put the program into

Simon Poidevin, one of Australian rugby's hardest trainers, working out under the program prepared for him by Frank Pyke. John Fairfax Group

action.

As expected, some players took to it much more easily than others. A few of our hardest trainers — Simon Poidevin and Jeff Miller are two who come immediately to mind — embraced the program eagerly. for it provided them with the kind of direction they had long been seeking. The young players who had already spent time at the Australian Institute of Sport accepted it happily, too, because to them it seemed quite natural. Some of the older players were not easily persuaded, but all came around in the end.

The program was highly structured and was specific for each player, depending on his size, physique, strength, stamina and metabolism. Here is how it worked. At the start of of December, a player would have a program mapped out for him for the months ahead. In weeks one to four he might have to run or swim certain distances each day, do strength-development exercises four times a week, work out in the gym five times a week, eat certain types of food in certain quantities according to sample menus, and so on. In weeks five to eight, the program would be modified slightly. In weeks nine to twelve it would be modified again, and so on. In addition, the players attended two off-season camps or workshops, at which they were lectured and counselled by experts on fitness, strength, phsyiology, nutrition, psychology and other areas. Naturally, the program was timed to bring the players to a state of match preparedness by the start of the Rugby season.

We were not too rigid about it. We weren't asking the players to train six hours a day, because that was unrealistic. We were simply saying that here was a program that could help them play better and this was how much time they needed to devote to it. If any player was unable to devote that amount of time to it, we were happy to look at the possibility of redesigning a program specially for him. It might not be the ideal program, but it might be the best that was possible under the circumstances. We were not setting goals for them. We were not saying that they had to achieve a specific degree of fitness and strength by a certain date. We were just providing them with a means of becoming fitter, stronger, tougher and smarter than they were now. I also assured them that whether or not they chose to follow the program closely would have no bearing at all on whether they were selected. Selections would be made solely on performance.

We also introduced what the experts call an 'individual performance assessment scheme'. I enlisted the services of a number of coaches, ex-coaches and ex-players who were capable of giving an objective evaluation of how each player was performing. They were assigned to assess each player's performance in a designated list of areas — set plays, loose plays, defence, attack, support, positional play, work rate, explosiveness and so on. In this way, we were able to monitor how each player was performing and identify his strengths and weaknesses.

The impact of all this on the team was dramatic. In some cases, the preparation program has changed the player's entire approach to the game. It has changed his understanding of how best to prepare for a game, his understanding of his body as a mechanical apparatus, his understanding of his own physiology. Our experience with the Australian team has confirmed my belief that education is itself a motivational tool. The more a player knows about his body, the better he trains, and the better he trains, the fitter and more powerful he becomes, which in turn encourages him to want to know more. This is why some of the Australian players absorbed the information faster than we could supply it.

On the field, the benefits of the program showed up in improved fitness, strength and explosiveness. The players' mental attitude was changed, too. Because they knew they had prepared themselves well, they played with more confidence. They really believed they were part of a top outfit. Another benefit, I have found, is that the players are more receptive to technical evaluations of their performance. In short, they have developed the mentality of the elite athlete who knows that it is the extra one per cent in performance which separates the best from second-best.

What I find enormously encouraging about all these developments is that we have so far scarcely scratched the surface of their potential. There is much more that we can do and, I am sure, will do. In 1990, our physiology team began a study of the running styles of our players. The aim was to study the movement of the lower back and pelvic girdle under acceleration, the pronation of the feet and the subsequent effect on the lower leg,

Jeff Miller . . . among the hardest trainers in the Australian squad.

Ross Setford

and the influence of the stomach muscles on the positioning of the pelvis, and so on. To the layman, this may all sound absurdly academic. In fact, it has an important bearing on every player's mechanical efficiency and his susceptibility to injury. One of the initial findings was that Simon Poidevin's strenuous fitness routine had caused a structural imbalance. Because of the kind of exercises Poidevin had been doing, it was found that his upper stomach muscles were relatively much stronger than his lower stomach muscles. This had the effect of rotating his pelvis, which, in turn, interfered with his natural running style and reduced his speed. Many more lessons of this kind are there for the learning.

16

DIRTY PLAY

The Lions who toured Australia in 1989 were at times the dirtiest team I have ever seen in international Rugby. I say this because their use of foul tactics was not occasional but was a common and consistent theme of their play. Significantly, the officials accompanying the team insisted we had nothing much to complain about. Sure, there had been a few isolated acts by players out of control, they said, but nothing more than this. One player, a Welsh prop, was certainly out of control. On one occasion, I saw him stomp on the side of Steve Cutler's head. On another occasion, I saw him try to stomp on Lloyd Walker's head. Walker whipped his face away just in time, yet he was still grazed from the corner of his eye down the side of his face. Ordinarily, I would say, 'There are crazy people everywhere. Just remove that crazy person from your team and everything will be all right.' The Lions were different. With them, dirty play was a persistent, deliberate, all-embracing tactic.

I do not know if the Lions' dirty play in 1989 was a planned strategy. If it was, I have no idea how or by whom the plan was conceived. There was a precedent for it, however. In 1974, after the touring Lions had comprehensively defeated South Africa in the Test series, it emerged they had worked out a plan beforehand to rough up the Springboks. I have been told that they even had a call, the number 'ninety-nine', which the team responded to by laying into the opposition. The strategy, it seems, was enormously successful. It happens that the Lions' coach in 1989, Ian McGeechan, and the assistant coach, Roger Uttley, were both players in that Lions team in 1974. I would find it hard to believe, however, that either would have stooped to devising tactics of this kind.

The Lions' dirty play in 1989 took many forms. When the front rows of the scrum collapsed, the Lions' second-rowers kicked their opponents in the head. This did not happen occasionally, but nearly every time the scrum folded. On one such occasion, as a second-rower swung back his boot, he smashed his own number-eight, Dean Richards, in the face with his heel and broke a tooth. Suspecting that the second-rower had intended to kick an Australian, we found it hard to feel sorry for Richards. For the first time in my life I saw a player jump on top of a referee. Nick Farr-Jones was on the ground scuffling with the Welsh scrum half, Robert Jones, who was on top of him, and the French referee bent down to separate them. As he did so, the Lions captain, Finlay Calder of Scotland, jumped on top of the referee, knocking him over, and then lay on top of the referee swinging punches at Farr-Jones. This may have been an isolated incident, but it was symptomatic of the Lions' general approach.

Nick Farr-Jones, chased by Finlay Calder and Wade Dooley, carrying the scars of a clash with the Lions during the bloody series of 1989.   Garry Taylor

After the series was over the Australian Rugby Union sent a letter of protest to Rugby authorities in Britain, enclosing a video which contained visual evidence of the dirty play complained about. I understand that Rugby authorities in Britain chose to ignore the complaint. A year or two later, one of the Lions players on that tour cast a revealing light on the affair while speaking to an Australian administrator. Asked about the foul play his team had engaged in, he said, 'It wasn't all of us. It was the English coppers.' This player, it goes without saying, was not an Englishman.

After the Lions won the second Test, the *Sydney Morning Herald* commentator Evan Whitton wrote in reference to them that 'the scum also rises.' This was indicative of the outrage Australian Rugby followers felt at the Lions tactics. Four Australian players required stitches after the second Test — Greg Martin, Michael Lynagh, Steve Tuynman and Nick Farr-Jones. Yet in the long term the Lions did us a favour. They exposed our vulnerability, mentally, to the kind of bully-boy tactics they employed. I had the feeling even before this that a number of the players who had played for Australia in the previous few years were not as hard-nosed as they needed to be. Some of these Test players, I knew, were not regarded as being tough players even in club Rugby. Usually, when club players meet a team containing two or three Test players they tend to feel a little intimidated by them. The appearance of a few of these Test players in a club match, however, was almost welcomed by the opposition.

As a result, there was a mental attitude prevailing in the Australian team in the late 1980s which made Australia a soft target for any team which set out to unsettle it with foul play. It is the unsettling effect of dirty play, rather than the cuts and bruises it causes, which is the cause of concern. For any team to perform well at any game, the players must have their minds focused on the play. Conversely, if their minds are distracted, they will not play so well. Dirty play can act as a distraction to the opposition, not so much because it makes them afraid of injury but simply because it makes them stop and think, 'What's all this about? Who started the fight? That bloke must be a madman.' In other words, they are distracted. Instead of moving forward with concentration, they're back on their heels with their eyes wide open wondering what is going on. The players responsible for the dirty play do not have the same disadvantage. On the contrary. If the dirty play is part of a preconceived plan, they will be more focused then usual. They will be thinking to themselves, 'Stage one is stomping on the opposition and hopefully provoking a response. If that causes a distraction, we will capitalise on it by moving to stage two and see if we can consolidate our advantage before the opposition has time to settle down.'

In the light of the Lions experience, the need to withstand this kind of tactic became one of our considerations when choosing players for the team. Ever since we have made sure that the people we chose were capable of taking and giving hard knocks without being put off their game. We have never forgotten the Lions of 1989. We learned our lesson. If the Lions had toured Australia two years later, in 1991, and tried the same approach, I feel confident they would have encountered a different kind of response.

Dirty play becomes a blot on the game when it becomes a *feature* of the game. In Britain, there have been incidents which received the widest coverage because they occurred in international matches. Quite apart from the injuries suffered by the victims, these incidents must have the effect of bringing the game into disrepute. One such incident occurred during the England-Scotland match in the 1992 Five Nations tournament. Wade Dooley felled Gordie Weir from behind with an elbow to the back of the head. This was not the first time I had seen this done. The Lions did the same thing in Australia a number of times in 1989. I saw one player have his head split open in this way. I can only assume that this kind of play has become an accepted part of the England armament.

There was another example of what I have been speaking about in the Scotland-Ireland pool match in the 1991 World Cup. The outcome of the match was in the balance when the Scots put up a high kick which was taken by the Irish fullback, Jim Staples. As he took it, Staples was caught in a legitimate tackle by one Scottish player and then felled by a swinging arm to the head by a second Scottish player following on. This second Scottish player was the flanker Finlay Calder, who I referred to earlier as the captain of the 1989 Lions in Australia. Staples was concussed by the blow and should really have left the field, because almost immediately Scotland put up another high ball to Staples, who dropped it. As a result

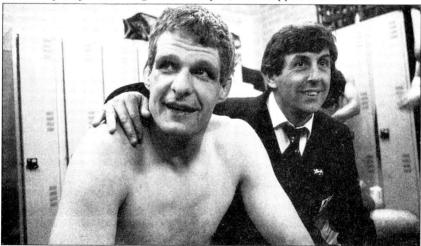

Finlay Calder, here with 1989 Lions coach Ian McGeechan, was involved in an unfortunate incident in the World Cup pool match between Scotland and Ireland.   Allsport

of this error by Staples, who no doubt was still suffering the effects of the earlier blow to the head, Scotland scored and went on to win the match.

I cannot understand why Rugby authorities in Britain have not taken steps to stamp out foul play. It is absurd to argue that the referee is in sole charge of the game and that if he doesn't take action there is nothing administrators can do. If an incident like the one I described, which is plainly outside the laws of the game, is allowed to occur without comment, players everywhere will be entitled to believe that Rugby authorities condone it. If such actions go unchecked, the sport as a whole will certainly suffer in the long term. How can players feel confident in playing to the limit of their ability if they think they are in danger of assault?

I am sure there is not as much dirty play today as there was twenty to thirty years ago when I was playing, but the game today is much faster than it was then, and perhaps for this reason the injuries inflicted by foul play seem to be worse. In other words, the acts of dirty play are fewer in number but more serious in nature. Foul play is still entrenched in the game. I have already spoken of teams which set out as a deliberate tactic to intimidate the opposition with foul play ranging from constant niggling to blatant acts of physical assault. Just as serious, if less reprehensible, are the individual acts of foul play performed by players overcharged with adrenalin. We are all familiar with the spectacle of players running on to the field in a hyper-aggressive state and commiting an act of foul play in the opening minutes of the match. There was a clear example of this, which I will describe in a later chapter, in the first few moments of Australia's quarter-final match against Ireland at the 1991 World Cup. An Australian was punched by an Irishman while the ball from the kick-off was still in the air.

There is a third and equally detestable category of dirty play. Here, the perpetrators are the crazy men of the game — callous players who seem incapable of preventing themselves performing various acts of atrocity throughout each match. I would like to be able to say that these tend to be inferior players who seek to make their mark by foul means because they cannot make it by fair means, but, unfortunately, this is not so. I have known some very good players over the years who were dirty players. If you had to categorise dirty players in some way, I suppose you could say they were usually forwards, which is not really surprising. After all, there is much less scope for backs to indulge in this kind of play and hope to get away with it. It has also been my impression that slower players are more likely to be dirty players, but I cannot suggest why this should be the case.

In my opinion, parochialism is one of the main problems to be overcome before we can deal properly with the issue of dirty play. People are outraged at the foul play of opposition teams, but they tend to either ignore entirely or take a very lenient view of foul play by their own players. What we need is a change in the culture of the game. We need to have it generally recognised that foul play detracts from the game and inhibits skill and flair. Anyone who wants to play the game with skill and flair ought to feel completely confident in doing so. They should not feel they run a risk of being punched or kicked or stomped on if, in the course of exercising their skill, they place themselves in a vulnerable position. I do not suggest that changing the culture of the game in this way will be easy, but if we all took a couple of deep breaths and really attacked the problem I believe we could make progress quite quickly. This would not only benefit the prospective victims of foul play. In my view, it would benefit the prospective perpetrators, because foul play is also a distraction to the players who perform it.

Some steps have already been taken. Previously, under the laws of the game, the referee has always been the sole arbiter of what happens on the field. This is changing. Already, anyone watching a Rugby game in New Zealand, whether at the ground or on television, can report an incident to the game's authorities. As a result, a number of players have been suspended, including Alan Whetton. In the centenary series there against a World XV in 1992, Rugby authorities took action after the public reported an incident in which the Australian player Brendan Nasser had his hand broken by a New Zealand player who stamped on it. These new measures are, in my view, steps in the right direction. They need to be supported by tougher penalties. Rugby League in Australia has shown us the way here. In recent years the League has imposed heavy penalties for deliberate acts of foul play, and we have seen offenders suspended for terms ranging from eight to eighteen weeks.

One difficulty faced by legislators is that there is a grey area between vigorous, aggressive play and blatantly dirty play. How referees view this grey area seems to vary from country to country. In New Zealand, for instance, it is considered quite fair and legal to ruck a player out of the way of the ball, and by and large a similar view prevails in Australia. The attitude is that if a player is lying on the ground on your side of the ball you are entitled to either ruck him out of the way or make life so uncomfortable for him that he will want to move of his own accord. In some other countries, rucking out a player in this way is considered deplorable. This different interpretation of the laws is one thing. What complicates it is the grey area. Where does rucking out end and stomping begin? I cannot think of any player who has been seriously hurt by being rucked out. Stomping is altogether different. I have seen stomping injuries so serious that it was hard to comprehend how they occurred. After Andrew Leeds was stomped on in a Test against New Zealand in 1988 he had a wound in the side of his head which looked like a bullet hole. He had a similar wound in his thigh with a savage tear beside it. Clearly, a New Zealander had punctured his leg right down to the muscle and then ripped the flesh away. Such an injury could not have been inflicted by someone trying to ruck Leeds out of the way. It was clearly the result of a deliberate, powerful stomp.

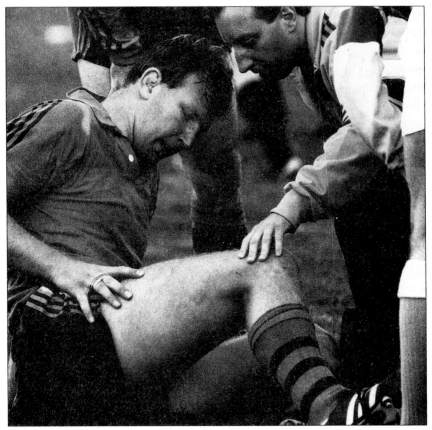

Steve Tuynman receives treatment during the second test against the Lions in 1989. He was one of four Australian players requiring stitches. Garry Taylor

Fortunately, more often than not, there is nothing personal in the physical damage which players inflict on each other. Some years ago the Sydney representative team was practising scrummaging against the Eastern Suburbs team. At that time, Declan Curran, an Australian player, was propping for Sydney, and one of his brothers, Frank, was playing second-row for Easts. The story goes that as the scrum packed down Frank Curran dropped his bind and shot a punch up through the scrum, hitting his brother in the face and splitting his eye open. The scrum erupted and Declan reeled out, holding his eye. The eye was bleeding profusely, and the Sydney coach, Peter Crittle, wanted Declan to go off and get it attended to, but Declan insisted on staying on, saying that a little blood never hurt anyone. So the scrum packed down again, whereupon Declan kicked Frank in the face. The background to this story is that the two brothers are as close as only brothers can be.

17

WINTER OF CONTENT

For me, the year 1991 really began in November 2, 1990. This was twelve months to the day before the final of World Cup. I phoned Nick Farr-Jones, who was in Adelaide at the time competing in a celebrity motor race, and told him to drink a glass of champagne that evening. He asked why, and I suggested he might like to toast our victory in the World Cup twelve months in advance. Farr-Jones promised that he would, and he later confirmed that he did. On that same day I made similar calls to several other players, Simon Poidevin, Michael Lynagh and Jeff Miller among them. Phil Kearns was working for me at the time, so we had a glass of champagne together.

The countdown to the World Cup had begun. Our first get-together as a team in 1991 was at a squad camp in January at the University of Queensland in Brisbane. In the previous year, we had started a squad of forty-five on the preparation program. By now, this number had been reduced to thirty-six. At this camp we did tests on the players to assess their current level of fitness. We measured their cardio-vascular fitness, anaerobic fitness, body strength, vertical and horizontal power, and level of body fat. On the basis of the results we revised the training program for the players for the next few weeks. We repeated the exercise at another camp in Sydney in February, and again a few months later. There were various kinds of fitness and coaching consultants at these camps, and the players had many discussions with them, usually individually.

At this early stage we also sorted out various house-keeping matters such as when and how players would be issued with gear, whether wives would be flown to Test venues, whether there would be a team dinner after matches, and so on. None of these things have anything to do with the playing of Rugby, of course, but the players tend to worry about them, so it is much better to get them out of the way as quickly as possible. I was once asked to speak to a group of businessmen on motivation. Pondering the subject beforehand, I came to the conclusion that what motivation really meant was providing an atmosphere in which a person could realise his or her full potential. By providing this atmosphere, you will do far more to motivate a Rugby player in the long term than by trying to generate a mood of fierce determination in the team just before a match. One way to provide this atmosphere is to unburden the player of any worries he may have about extraneous matters such as what plane his wife is arriving on, whether there will be anyone at the airport to meet her, whether the ticket to the match will be waiting for her at the hotel. These incidentals are necessarily a distraction to players needing to concentrate on match preparation. If a wife can look forward to being flown on Saturday morning to a home Test, seeing the match in the afternoon, attending a team dinner afterwards and looking over the town on Sunday before flying home, she will live much more happily with the fact that her husband plays Rugby — and so will he.

When I surveyed our prospects as we approached the start of the 1991 season, it seemed to me that we were capable of defeating Wales, England and New Zealand in Australia but that we might find it hard to defeat New Zealand in the return Test in New Zealand. After that, I thought we were a strong chance in the World Cup, by which I mean that we were *capable* of winning it. I believed our players possessed the basic ability to do it, and that this ability would be enhanced by the type of preparation the team had undergone, which I felt sure was the best in the world. I also knew that we had a stronger off-field support system than ever before.

There were a few other reasons for optimism. In the previous year we had unearthed a couple of exceptional players. One was Willie Ofahengaue, who clearly had the capacity to become a powerful force in the side. Speed and power are the keys to the modern game. Expressed another way, it is the optimum combination of weight and acceleration which makes a player effective. In Ofahengaue, we had a player who possessed both size and acceleration. If you sent him on a 3000-metre run he would be stricken with exhaustion, yet he had the ability to generate tremendous power in short bursts. Another player who had come to light in 1990 was John Eales. There were some influential people who thought Eales was an outstanding prospect yet felt he was not ready for Test selection. 'What a pity the World Cup's not being played in 1992,' one of them said to me. 'Eales would be just about right by then.' I did not believe a word of it.

So, as in 1984, when Topo Rodriguez and Nick Farr-Jones materialised out of nowhere, two fine players had dropped into our laps. On the other hand, we were missing the service of the winger John Flett, who had proved to be a player of quality in New Zealand in 1990 but who had been injured badly and was not back to his best. This was compensated for by the emergence of another fine winger, Rob Egerton. Egerton was a player whose particular talents fitted the needs of the team almost perfectly. He was like the jigsaw piece that completes the puzzle. He was a great chaser of the ball, a tenacious defender and a good catcher, and he played with concentration. These qualities of his and the explosiveness of Campese on the other wing made an effective combination. Egerton was not slow, either. He demonstrated this by defeating the speedy Michael O'Connor by some distance in a beach sprint at Manly in Sydney.

With the World Cup in view, all the players were fit, keen and available. Recognising this, some of the Rugby journalists wrote optimistically about our chances in the World Cup, dwelling on the fact that Australia had unusual depth in various positions. I saw these comments and drew the players' attention to them. I said that depth, of itself, was worthless. There was no benefit to be gained from having a group of good players of roughly equal ability to choose from for each position.

Rob Egerton . . . the ideal replacement for John Flett.

What we needed was at least one world-class player in each position. I told the team that when people started choosing world XVs after the World Cup I wanted every member of the Australian team to be at least considered a candidate in his particular position. This was not the case at present, I said, so there was no comfort to be drawn from what the press had to say. They were good, I told them, but not good enough. There was still a lot of work to do.

There were a number of gaps and weaknesses to work on. We needed to improve our second-row performance, especially in general play. In the set plays, we were probably good enough. Fullback was a problem, too. One option was to play Campese there, but our first choice was to play him on the wing, so it became a priority to find a fullback of quality. We needed to find a second winger, given that Flett was in doubt, and we also needed to work out our best back-row combination. Most of these problems were solved early on when Eales, Marty Roebuck and Egerton came to the fore.

The first Test we played in 1991 was against Wales. We won by 63 to 6, and we played fairly well to do it. Then we played England, the reigning Five Nations champion. I expected this to be a tough contest, and I knew we would have to play well to win. In fact, Australia played possibly the best eighty minutes of Rugby I have ever seen an Australian team play. We won 40 to 15, a result which I think stunned people in the English camp. Several of the English commentators, having witnessed their team take such a beating, were prepared to write off England's chances in the World Cup there and then. The theme of their remarks was that this match had turned their worst fears into reality, that even though England had won the Five Nations tournament it was obviously a class below the best in the world. The England players were too slow, they said. They lacked flair, and they lacked vision.

I regard that performance highly because of the *precision* of our play. Many commentators like to speak of Australia playing with flair in attack and playing an expansive, fifteen-man game. This has produced a false image in people's minds. I once said to someone that I would not like the type of Rugby Australia plays to be likened to a frilly evening dress. I would much prefer it to be likened to a well-tailored suit, cut with precision from the best cloth, nicely structured and devoid of any trimmings. That was certainly the type of game we played against England. Everything we did was done with precision. It was text-book Rugby — sharp, neat, efficient, structured. I said before that it was possibly the best I have seen any Australian team play. I hesitate to say more than this because it is extremely difficult to compare performances against teams of varying strengths. I have seen Australia play wonderfully well in a Test, only to hear people write off the performance later on the grounds that the opposition must obviously have been weak since the score was so high. What I can say with certainty is that we played better against England that day than in any other match in 1991, including the matches we played in the World Cup.

Our third Test of the home season was against the All Blacks. Again, we played well and won well. The score was 21 to 12. For me, a heartening feature of this performance against New Zealand was the dominance of our forwards. We were so clearly the better side on the day that even the most pessimistic of Rugby followers in Australia began to recognise that Australia really did have a chance of winning the World Cup.

Thus ended what had been a hugely successful winter in Australia. Our wins over Wales, England and New Zealand, following on our victory in the last Test against New Zealand the year before, resulted in an upturn of popular interest in the team. Australians at large began to feel that here was a team of real quality which looked to be headed for greater things. I could sense that public enthusiasm was building up. This was evident even in the way the spectators sang the national anthem before the Tests. Never in living memory had any group of Australians sung the anthem with so much passion. This stirring of national pride in the team showed up in other ways. A group of people calling themselves the Wallabies Supporters Group began holding a luncheon in the week before each Test, for

It's not often the Wallabies beat the All Blacks, and do it in style. Such occasions are worth celebrating. John Fairfax Group

Tony Daly salutes Australia's marvellous 21-12 victory over the All Blacks in Sydney in 1991. His team mates are a little more subdued. There were bigger goals ahead.   John Fairfax Group

instance. The players themselves sensed this growing mood of support and, I think, were lifted by it.

After that, we went to New Zealand to play a return Test and, we hoped, win the Bledisloe Cup. For once, our well-organised system of pre-match preparation failed to work efficiently. There were many small irritations on and off the field. To begin, there was uncertainty about which hotels we would be staying in. Then we found that our training ground was water-logged and that there was a mix-up over what type of ball would be used in the match. There was also confusion about the number of footballs issued to us for training and about the supply of other gear. These were all minor matters, but I was conscious at the time of a general feeling in the team that things were not running smoothly.

On top of this, I was disappointed by the way the backs were training in admittedly difficult conditions, and I found it hard to get our mid-field players, in particular, to adjust to the way I wanted them to play. I had some harsh words to say to the backs at training, which were overheard by some of the press people there. I was very frank with the press. I told them I was not happy with our preparation and that I had some misgivings about the coming Test. Don Cameron, one of New Zealand's best-known Rugby writers, told me I was sounding like the Bob Dwyer of old who, he said, used to try to 'con' New Zealanders into thinking that the Australians were not up to standard. In fact, I was simply being truthful.

We played badly in the Test at Auckland and lost by 6 points to 3. Our discipline was poor. We allowed ourselves to be rattled under pressure, and we also let the New Zealanders off the hook when we had them under pressure in the last twenty minutes of the match. Afterwards, there was a lot of criticism of the referee by the press. The main reason for the criticism was that the referee repeatedly halted the play to award penalties to one or other of the teams. My own view is that the criticism was largely unjustified. Occasionally I thought the penalty went the wrong way, but for the most part I thought the referee was justified in stopping the play when he did. There had been a lot of rain before the Test, and the playing conditions that day were so difficult that errors were inevitable. If a knock-on by one team is followed by a knock-on by the opposition, the referee has no option but to stop play. He cannot play the advantage. There were many instances of this and similar errors throughout the match.

The most disappointing feature of our play was that we failed to play a controlled game in the last twenty minutes or so of the match, when we were right on top and had New Zealand under intense pressure in their own quarter and often within a few metres of the line. On a number of occasions we tried to score when a try was clearly not on, and we made one fly shot at a field-goal, always a high-risk option on a muddy pitch. On another occasion, one of our players was penalised for striking an opponent, which at once relieved the pressure on the New Zealanders. If the victim of the incident had been asked beforehand whether he was prepared to take a blow in the face in return for a penalty, I am sure he would have happily agreed.

With hindsight, it can be argued that the loss of this Test to New Zealand was a blessing for us in the long term. If we had not lost to the New Zealanders then, perhaps we may have lost to them in the semi-final of the World Cup. The important thing about this match was that we played badly and lost. If we had played badly and won, as we nearly did, I am sure it would have given us a false idea of how things stood. I told the players afterwards to forget about the scoreboard and just examine the way they played. We studied a video of the match. The backs were much too far apart, as they had been all week in training; this pass was slightly askew, causing the receiver to slip over; here, we were panicked by an urge to score, whereas we should have maintained control of the play and kept the opposition pinned down. Thus, we were compelled by defeat to refocus our attention on the things we ought to have done and had succeeded in doing in the Test against England. In particular, I was able to show the players how they had allowed the scoreboard to influence the way they played in those last twenty minutes. I had been urging them for years not to allow this to happen, and I think the loss to New Zealand really drove the lesson home.

The loss to New Zealand was a blessing in another way. It convinced the New Zealanders that after losing twice to us in consecutive games they had now rediscovered the secret. In fact, we all thought the New Zealand-

Tim Horan, shadowed by Mark Carter, about to throw a pass during the second 1991 Bledisloe Cup encounter at Eden Park. Andrew Cornaga, Photosport

ers played badly in the Auckland Test, but because the scoreboard at the end of the match read 6-3 in their favour their performance was praised by the New Zealand media. New Zealand had drawn the series and retained the Bledisloe Cup. For most New Zealanders, this was enough to be thankful for.

18

THE ROAD TO TWICKENHAM

Our World Cup campaign received what some Australians considered a mortal blow during the two weeks that separated the two New Zealand Tests in 1991. There was a spare weekend in this period, and Tim Gavin was prevailed upon to play in a club match for his club, Eastern Suburbs. I have been told he was carrying a slight injury beforehand and was reluctant to play, but, being the fine team man that he is, agreed to turn out. Tim injured his knee in the match. I was notified about it immediately afterwards, although at that stage it seemed he had suffered no more than a strain. I phoned the team's physiotherapist, Greg Craig, and described the symptoms to him. He said it sounded to him worse than a strain, but he reserved judgment until he had examined Gavin himself. I was attending a family party that evening, but I gave him the phone number. He phoned me there that night to say Gavin had ruptured a cruciate ligament, one of the most serious injuries a player can sustain. It requires a major operation and a long period of rehabilitation. The calamitous news was that Gavin was not only out of the return Test against New Zealand but was out of the World Cup, too.

We were leaving the next day for New Zealand, so we had to arrange a hasty replacement. This was the immediate concern, but already I was looking beyond this to the World Cup. Gavin would not easily be replaced. We needed a number-eight forward of international quality who was capable of filling the jumping position at number-six in the lineout. New South Wales B had played such a forward that season, Steve Tuynman, but Queensland and the ACT had not. All the flankers for the New Zealand tour had been picked, and none of them could fill the jumping position, so all we could do was experiment again, just as we had with Gavin a few years earlier. The tragedy, both for Gavin and Australia, was that Gavin was having his best season ever and had been a dominant force in our Test victories that season. After we arrived in Britain for the World Cup a few months later and watched videos of the home Tests we

Tim Gavin in control at a lineout against the All Blacks in Sydney in 1991.
A week later he so badly damaged his knee in a club fixture he didn't play
again for six months.   Photosport

won that year against England and New Zealand, it became even more
obvious how much Gavin had contributed to those successes and how big
were the shoes his replacement needed to fill. Happily, the occasion found
the man, Troy Coker, who was to play a significant role in our ultimate
victory.

A year or more before we left for Britain I had spoken to Australian
Rugby officials about the need for a quiet, out-of-the-way base in Britain,
where we could prepare for the World Cup matches. The Rothmans
national director of coaching, Dick Marks, had checked out a couple of
possibilities. Our first choice was a place in Wales, but this was not
available. In any case, we learned that we had to be in London for an
opening World Cup dinner, so it was decided we base ourselves at the
Lensbury Club outside London. This was a club maintained by the Shell
company for the use of its employees, and it was surrounded by vast
grounds. The Australian team had trained there before, and it was known
to be private and to have excellent facilities, including several beautifully
surfaced Rugby fields, a dozen tennis courts, croquet courts, squash courts,
a gym, swimming pool, kayaks and canoes. We moved in, and without
much encouragement from me the team began training with such a fierce
earnestness that Joe French, the president of the Australian Rugby Union,
told me he had never seen a Rugby team train as hard. In fact, the team's
physiotherapist and sports physiologist were both beginning to warn of a
risk of over-use injuries when I decided the team had to taper off anyway
in preparation for our move to Wales for the opening match against
Argentina.

By now, we were starting to have a closer look at the opposition. New
Zealand and England still seemed to us to be the biggest threats, although
because of the nature of the draw I gave Scotland a chance of making it to

the final. Despite the draw, I did not rule out the possibility of an Australia-New Zealand final altogether, because I thought England had a chance of beating New Zealand in the first round of the competition. On the other hand, I doubted England's ability to win their way through to the final via Paris and Murrayfield. There was a good chance it would win one of the matches, against either France or Scotland, but it was clearly a tough assignment for England to win both.

In recent years we had done a lot of detailed research on opposition teams. It was so detailed, in fact, that we were usually able to identify the strengths and weaknesses of most individual players opposing us. I described earlier how a player-assessment scheme had been set up in Australia, under which a group of people knowledgeable about the game regularly observed and then reported on each elite player's performance in a number of areas of the game. Before the World Cup, we applied this same expertise to reporting on opposing teams. An extremely capable team of three — Dick Marks, David Clark and Brian O'Shea — was assigned to study videos of matches involving teams we were likely to play and report to me on what they saw. They did a lot of this before we left Australia and continued doing it in Britain when the World Cup tournament got under way. By this means, I was supplied with some very useful and up-to-date information about our opponents, which I then assessed and used to shape our tactics.

Before the tournament began, we considered ourselves to be playing in the toughest pool. Our opponents would be, in order, Argentina, Western Samoa and Wales. Of the countries we had been drawn to play, I rated Argentina the biggest danger. Australia had never found it easy to beat Argentina, and certainly not outside Australia. Argentina had slipped a little over the previous ten years or so, but as recently as 1987 had defeated Australia in a series in Argentina. The Argentinians could be expected to be a physically strong, tough-tackling team. Whatever the result, we knew it would not be an easy match.

We knew a good deal about the Argentinians, and we also knew quite a lot about the Western Samoans. We were not at all surprised by the success they went on to achieve at the World Cup, for we had seen them in action many times at the Hong Kong Sevens competition. Moreover, many of them were based in New Zealand, and we knew how vigorously they played. If you go to Hong Kong and find you are in the same pool as the Western Samoans, you groan inwardly and wonder how you will line up for the next match, for they play a very tough game. Wales was an uncertain proposition. We had thrashed the Welsh in Australia only a few months before, but we guessed they would have changed their team and that, in any case, they would be harder to beat at home. Moreover, we calculated that they would be determined to make amends for the crushing defeat we inflicted on them in what was their off-season.

The road to Twickenham was plainly not going to be downhill.

19

SO FAR SO GOOD

We went to Llanelli in Wales for our first match against Argentina. We won by 32 to 19. The match proved to be as tough physically as we expected, but we were in control for most of the game, notwithstanding the fact that in the second half the Argentinians narrowed the gap to 4 points. I could not remember when we last scored as many as five tries against Argentina, but our satisfaction at this was partly offset by the fact the Argentinians had scored two tries against us. This was disappointing, because we rated defence as one of the chief strengths of our game. In fact, in all four Tests we had played against Wales, England and New Zealand earlier in the year the opposition had managed to cross our line only twice. On the whole, however, it was a pleasing opening for us. Phil Kearns left the field with a knee injury, but happily the injury was not found to be serious.

One problem remained unresolved — how best to fill the number-eight position left vacant by Tim Gavin. We experimented in this match by putting John Eales there. Although Eales had played all his senior representative Rugby at second row and had been excelling in this position, he had nevertheless played more often at number-eight over the whole of his career. The experiment was not successful. Eales shaped up well in some respects, but he was certainly no Tim Gavin.

The next game was against Western Samoa, which was fresh from a victory over Wales at Cardiff, not an inconsiderable achievement. At the start of the tournament, a large section of the Australian team had gone four to six weeks without playing a match. When we sat down to choose the side to play Western Samoa, we were conscious of the need to give players outside the 'first XV' match practice. We reasoned that if we failed to do this, and if we later had to call upon them as reserves for, say, the semi-final or final, they would by then have gone almost two months without playing a match.

The match was to be played at Pontypool. Two days beforehand we

Above: John Eales, being tried as a number-eight, ensures possession is retained during the World Cup opener against Argentina at Llanelli. Below: Jeff Miller leads a Wallaby raid against Western Samoa in the Pontypool murk.   Andrew Cornaga, Photosport

were invited to a reception there, which gave us a chance to look over the ground. What we saw alarmed us. Not only was the ground uneven, but there was a pronounced slope both across the field and down the field. The grandstand, changing rooms and other facilities were hardly up to international standard, either, although this did not particularly concern us. For all that, the setting was delightful. The ground was set in a lovely park, surrounded by beautiful trees resplendent in their autumn colours. It would have been a charming place to play a game of social Rugby, but the fact that the winning or the losing of the World Cup might be decided here was to the say the least unsettling. Nor did it help the players' state of mind when they ran on to the field to see the scoreboard reading 'Pontypool v Visitors'. We had no idea which of the two names represented Australia until we opened the scoring and saw a figure '3' had been placed beside Pontypool.

It would have been easy to regard this as whimsical and laugh it off, but I saw it as indicative of an unprofessional attitude among local Rugby authorities. After all, they had known for a long time that Australia and Western Samoa would be playing a World Cup match here, and it seemed to me that somebody might have taken the trouble to at least have the names of the teams posted on the scoreboard. There were other examples of second-rate organisation. I know of people who had travelled many thousands of kilometres to see the match only to find that their reserved seats had been taken and that officials at the ground could not care less. My wife, Ruth, had this experience. She and a friend had driven into Pontypool well before the match but were directed to a parking area beyond the outskirts of the town. The idea was that a shuttle bus would take people from the carpark to the ground. In fact, the bus did not turn up, so they had to walk for forty-five minutes in the rain to get to the ground, only to be told there were no grandstand seats left. The fact she had obtained grandstand tickets before she left Australia was immaterial. An official told her, simply, that she should have arrived earlier. After some argument, Ruth and her friend watched the match sitting in an aisle.

The people of Pontypool, I gather, were critical of me for being critical of the way the match was organised. They should understand that when players are surrounded by problems and confusion before a match their mental approach to the game must be affected. We had worked for too long and had come too far to let this happen.

We won the match by 9 to 3, which I suppose was a satisfactory ending to the Pontypool experience. The score suggests the contest was fairly close, yet if we had lost this match I think we could have counted ourselves most unlucky. We were really the only team which looked like scoring a try. Before the match, word had reached us that the Western Samoans were resigned to losing. They had worked out they could reach the quarter-finals by beating the other two teams in the pool, Wales and Argentina, so they had decided to field only a second-string team against Australia. Or so we were told. I asked the person who passed the information on to me: 'Do you really believe this? Do you know any Western Samoans?' I knew plenty of them, and I had no doubt they would go into the match against Australia at full strength and with a fierce determination to down one of the competition's hot favourites. This is what they tried to do.

We suffered one serious setback: Nick Farr-Jones injured his knee and was taken off. It happened during a planned move, which Farr-Jones had not played according to plan. When I asked him why later, he said he saw other players were not in position to go on with the move, so he decided to improvise. He turned back inside to pass the ball, and one of the Western Samoans hit him while he was off balance and twisted him

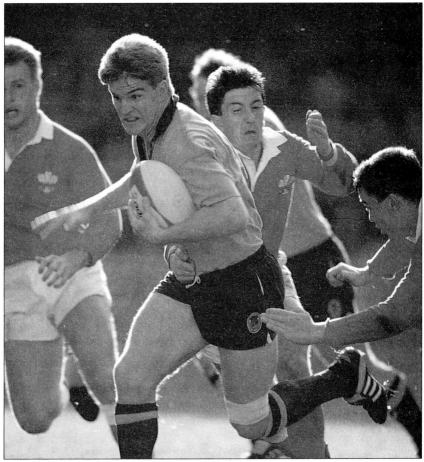

Tim Horan challenging the Welsh defences during the pool match at Cardiff. We won the game 38 to 3 but I wasn't happy with our back play.

Andrew Cornaga, Photosport

around, and he fell across his knee. It remained to be seen how disabling the injury was.

We moved to Cardiff to play Wales. In the days before the match I called on the team to lift its performance. I sensed the team had been coasting until then, apparently believing that when the time came and it found itself opposed by New Zealand or England it would be able to move into a higher gear. But this is not how things happen. No team in any sport can produce a top performance at will, as if by throwing a switch. A top performance is the result of a honing of skills. It was also clear that Wales' new coach, Alan Davies, was exhorting his team to pull out all stops against Australia. Wales desperately needed a strong showing in this match to redeem itself for its first-round loss to Western Samoa and for its heavy defeat in Australia earlier in the year.

When we left our hotel in central Cardiff to board the bus taking us to the ground, we were astonished to find a dense crowd of spectators in the street outside. I imagine there must have been as many as a thousand people there, and the police had to make a pathway through them to allow us to walk from the front door of the hotel to the bus. The Welsh passionately wanted their team to win that day, and I suppose they viewed us as the enemy, yet the mood of the crowd outside the hotel could not have been more friendly. They slapped the Australian players on the back and applauded us as we boarded the bus. Under the circumstances, I think we were all rather touched by this.

We won the match by 38 to 3 and performed well in certain areas, but our backs continued to play below their best. Australia enjoyed a glut of possession in the first half, yet at half-time our lead was only 10-3 and Wales was still in the match, which was a reflection on the inferior play of our backs. Our forwards did play well, though. They won the lineouts by twenty-four to two, which is the biggest lineout majority I have heard of in international Rugby. As a team we played with more purpose in the second half and ran up an impressive score, which most commentators took as a sign that all was well with the Australian campaign. I knew all was not well, however. After the Wales match, I felt obliged to read the riot act to the backs — and to a couple of them in particular. Essentially, my criticism was that the backs were not complying with the structure of mid-field play as we had set it out. It was our mid-field's responsibility to absorb as much of the opposition's defence as possible and so create opportunities for others in support play, or phase play, or out wide. Instead, they were trying to do the lot themselves. I kept saying to them, over and over, that the more often they were tackled the better.

So far so good. We now had a week to prepare for our quarter-final match against Ireland in Dublin. It was a week in which we would concentrate on improving the performance of our backs. As things turned out, it was a week well spent.

DESTINY IN DUBLIN

Only a few of our touring party had been to Ireland before, and they assured us before we arrived there that it was a delightful place full of delightful people. By the time we left, none of us would have disagreed with that. Like many other Australians who go there, we found that the disposition of the Irish was in many ways the same as our own. Dublin was a place where we all felt at home. More important, it was a place where we won two stirring victories.

The fact that we all expected to win well against Ireland was for me a cause of concern. The Irish have a way of lulling you into a false sense of security. You suspect it is a sham, yet they do it so well that perhaps it is all quite genuine. The Irish media and Irish Rugby followers spoke of our victory as if we had already won it. 'Now, don't be too hard on our boys,' people said to us. 'Try not to win by more than forty points.' The theme of everything being said and written was that Ireland had done well to make the quarter-finals and that it had to be satisfied with that. Even then, many Irish were assuring me they would be on our side when we played New Zealand in the semi-final. The possibility of their team being in the semi-final instead of us did not seem to occur to them.

In the week before the match I had the backs working very hard on a few specific moves which I thought might prove useful. One or two of these moves were practised a hundred times, literally, before I was satisfied the backs had mastered them. As coach, I have always held the view that if players cannot perform a move *perfectly* at training, when there is no opposition, they have no hope at all of performing it successfully in a match. The effort was not wasted. We scored two tries against Ireland using one of the moves we had practised, and one of these tries saved us the match.

The knee injury Nick Farr-Jones suffered in the match against Western Samoa kept him out of the Wales match and Peter Slattery played in his place. Farr-Jones returned for this match against Ireland but injured the

*Our captain Nick Farr-Jones limps out of the World Cup quarter-final in
Dublin. Luckily, in Peter Slattery we had a halfback well qualified to take over.*

Photosport

same knee early in this match. Slattery took his place again and played extremely well. The Ireland match suited Slattery's game. He was at his best scampering around the scrum. He was a fine broken-field runner, good at dodging, darting and flitting. He was also tough. He tackled hard and he was prepared to scramble for the ball. He was such a fine player that I think Nick Farr-Jones has always felt a little guilty about keeping him out of the Australian team, as if he were somehow to blame. I do know that one of the reasons Farr-Jones considered limiting his Rugby to club games in 1992 was that he thought Slattery deserved a regular place in the team. I may say it is typical of Farr-Jones' generosity of spirit that he should feel this way.

I suppose the Ireland Test will be remembered as a match we nearly lost, rather than a match we just won. It was an unusual contest in some respects. It certainly had an unusual beginning. Marty Roebuck kicked off to start the match, and in customary fashion the Australian forwards chased the ball. As Willie Ofahengaue, who was on the in-field side of the forward pack, ran past Ireland's captain, Phil Matthews, Matthews punched him in the side of the head. At this moment, it is worth remembering, the ball was still in the air from the kick-off. Thus we had the astonishing situation in which one player had attacked another before the ball had actually been touched in play. I had never seen Willie punch anyone on the Rugby field before, but I saw him now punching Matthews, who was forced to cover up. By this time a general melee had ensued, and in the midst of this another Irish player, Neil Francis, decided to come to Matthews's aid by punching Willie, whereupon Willie set upon him, too.

It was an act of foolhardiness on Francis's part, because Ofahengaue is an immensely powerful puncher. I know this because punching is one of the exercises we use to improve the players' upper-body endurance. Players take it in turns to put on gloves and spend a specified number of minutes punching a tackle shield held by a team-mate. Although the tackle shields are made of solid rubber and are as much as twenty centimetres thick, one player who held the shield while Willie was punching it said to me later: 'Thank goodness you called time when you did. I wanted to move my arm because I thought Willie was going to break it with the force of his punches through the shield, but I knew for sure that if I moved it he'd definitely break my ribs.' Phil Matthews is actually a likeable person, and at the dinner after the match Simon Poidevin said to him: 'You should have spoken to me before the match about the punch you were going to throw, because I could have told you who not to hit.' Someone else asked Matthews why he did it. He replied that he didn't really know — that he simply felt pumped-up and somehow it happened. It was an example of the adrenalin-driven aggression I referred to in an earlier chapter.

After this initial excitement, the match proper got under way. For the first seventy-odd minutes it did not occur to me we might lose, for we

Fullback Marty Roebuck draws two Irish defenders and passes to an unmarked Tim Horan during the stirring World Cup quarter-final at Lansdowne Road. We eventually won the game 19 to 18. Photosport

seemed to have things in control. The problem was that we were unable to pull away from them. We moved to 6-nil, and they levelled at 6-6. We moved to 9-6, and they levelled at 9-9. We moved to 15-9, and they closed the gap to 15-12. The main problem was that our forwards were not playing at all well. The lack of tightness in our lineout was deplorable. This allowed the Irish forwards to keep coming through after the ball — and sometimes in front of the ball. I think the referee may have been influenced by the predictions in the Irish press of an easy Australian victory, for he seemed to give the Irish plenty of leeway around the fringes of the play. All this while, I sensed that the team believed it could simply score a try if it found itself in danger.

Then came the Irish try five minutes before full-time. It was very well executed. We drifted across and had the right number of defenders, but Ireland put a grubber kick through and capitalised on it. The try showed up a lack of cover defence. In this Test we played the back row which we hoped to take into the semi-finals and final — Simon Poidevin and Jeff Miller as flankers and Willie Ofahengaue as number-eight, which is where he plays for his club. This was the most mobile back row we had available, yet the cover defence was not there. In fact, it was Rob Egerton from the other wing who tackled the Irish try-scorer, Gordon Hamilton, as he went over the line.

Suddenly, with only a few minutes of play left, Ireland had hit the front. The Irish crowd screamed with joy. Like other Australians in the grand-

Above: In what may have been the finest moment of his career, Michael Lynagh crosses for the matchwinning try against Ireland. He'd told his forwards if they pressured Ireland and won possession, the backs would score. They did. Below: Oh, the relief! 'Noddy' Lynagh allows himself to relax, knowing he'd taken his country through to the World Cup semi-finals. Photosport

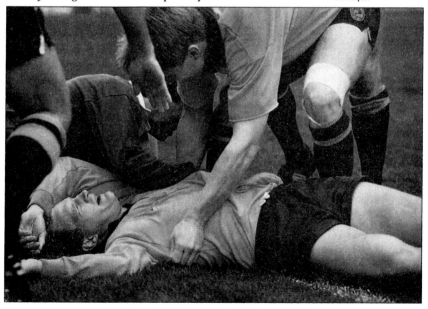

stand I was momentarily stunned. I remember thinking to myself, 'Surely, we aren't going to lose. Surely it's not all going to end here.' When we collected our thoughts, we realised not all was lost. The feeling on the bench was that we had enough time to do something about it, and I later learned that this was also the attitude of our captain,. Michael Lynagh, on the field. The Irish players assumed they had won, and who could blame them? I have been told that while they waited for the conversion attempt the Irish players spoke among themselves about their prospects against New Zealand in the semi-final a week later, although I very much doubt the truth of this.

Lynagh's composure at this point was critical. It may well have been the finest moment of his career. He told the Australian forwards he would kick off deep and that it was up to them to keep the Irish down at that end and win possession. If they won possession, he said, the backs would score. This is what they did. Lynagh himself scored two minutes before full-time and Australia won the match.

The try was a fairly standard move but it happened to be one of the moves we had practised endlessly during the previous week. The ball went from Slattery the half-back to Lynagh the five-eighth and then on to Horan the inside-centre. Horan passed to Roebuck the fullback, cutting out the outside-centre Little, who looped around to take the ball from Roebuck and pass it on to Campese the winger. Campese was tackled but as he was going down he managed to toss up the ball to Lynagh, who went over for the try. The move almost came unstuck because Little was held back without the ball by an Irish defender, Brendan Mullin, and it was only Lynagh's brilliant intervention at the end which made the try possible. If Little had not been held back, I have no doubt that Campese would have scored himself. Australia had scored a try with exactly the same move, in exactly the same position on the field, earlier in the same half, and on this occasion Campese scored the try as planned. In fact, the same Irish defender tried to hold Little back without the ball then, too, but Little was able to shrug him off.

Having had their spirits raised to the heavens six minutes before full-time, the Irish had now had them dashed. This dramatic reversal must have been awfully disappointing for them, but they bore it with remarkably good grace. Immediately after the match, an Irish official came up to me and said, 'Congratulations, Bob. You were far the better team.' I turned to Bob Templeton a moment later and said, 'Did you hear what he said? I couldn't have said that. Even if I thought it, I wouldn't have been able to get the words out.'

Weeks later, when I returned to Australia, someone I know in Sydney told me that in the early hours of the morning, after he and a few friends had watched the end of the Ireland match on television, there was a loud hammering on his front door. He opened the door to find his neighbour standing there, armed with a shovel. It emerged that the neighbour, having heard the whooping and screaming that erupted when Lynagh went over for the winning try, concluded that someone in the house was being assaulted.

I have watched a video of the Ireland Test several times since the World Cup, and when I watch those last few minuites I still feel my nerves knot in my stomach. They were certainly in a knot that day in Dublin. Nick Farr-Jones, who had come off the field injured, was sitting in front of me. Immediately after the final whistle, he turned to me and said, 'I honestly don't know how you can do this game after game, Bob. The pressure is incredible.' I believe the courage and composure the team displayed in saving the Ireland match was itself a big boost to our morale. Having done that, the Australians felt eager to take on the All Blacks.

By this time, we were being avalanched at each hotel with faxes and cards from Australia. By and large, the people who sent them simply wished us luck and said they would be watching and cheering for us. Some said they would also be praying for us. A few sent messages from unusual places, such as Australian bases in the Antarctic. A few others — presumably young women — sent messages offering sexual favours to the players once they returned to Australia. One or two of these made a point of urging the players not to waste their time on girls they met in Britain, who, they insisted, were much inferior. It was, I suppose, a kind of long-range jealousy.

I know it meant a lot to the players to know that so many people at home were supporting them. We are, unashamedly, a patriotic group. We sing the national anthem at all team meetings, for instance, and, furthermore, it is accepted that the players always meet certain standards of decorum when the anthem is sung. Jackets must be worn, ties done up, drinks put aside, and so on.

The backs had played pretty well in the Ireland match, but the forwards were disappointing. In assessing the match with the players, I raised the question of whether this was really the great Australian forward pack which had made such an impact on world Rugby that same year. Our forward play had been scrappy and loose, and the forwards themselves readily admitted this. During the following week they underwent special training sessions. They set goals for themselves before each session began, and when the session was over they discussed whether the goals had been achieved. They threw themselves into it with vigour, so much so that during one session one player reeled out of a maul accusing another of eye-gouging. I am sure it was accidental, but at least it showed they were in earnest. It certainly broke the tension, for the other forwards fell about laughing at the vehemence of the accusation.

Then, the big test — the semi-final against New Zealand. It was the match of the tournament at least as far the bookmakers were concerned, for it was between the two teams which they thought most likely to win. We decided that we needed changes, believing that we could not beat the All Blacks with the team which scraped through against Ireland. One selector was definite on this point. 'If we choose that same forward pack,' he said, 'we will be presenting the match to New Zealand.' In particular, we knew that we could not allow New Zealand to dominate us at the back of the lineout. Reluctantly, we left Jeff Miller out of the team and replaced him with Troy Coker. We knew Coker had played well at number-eight for Queensland against Auckland and Wellington earlier in the season, when Sam Scott-Young was injured, and, of course, he had played number-eight in the second Test that year against New Zealand. He had not been too impressive then, but it had been a tough, first-up assignment in a tough match.

Nick Farr-Jones was back in the team. Twice now he had come off the field with the same knee injury. We could only hope that he could see this match through.

I thought our forward play in the first thirty minutes of this semi-final was the best I have ever seen by an Australian team. Our forwards simply smashed the All Blacks into submission. It was significant that our first try came from a win at the back of the lineout, for this was the area we recognised as crucial. Our aim was to attack the New Zealand defence aggressively, and we did it here. John Eales took the ball at number-six in the lineout and Nick Farr-Jones put Michael Lynagh over the advantage line, after which David Campese ran left from the blind wing. Lynagh must have got seven metres over the advantage line, which is remarkable for a five-eighth, and this threw the All Blacks' defence into disarray.

Campese was brilliant. He scored the try running across the face of the defence. There were plenty of defenders in front of him, but because of the angle at which Campese was running they were all afraid to chase him, lest he gave a scissors pass to one of the Australians running outside him, or cut back inside himself. So each of the defenders played safe by making sure he had his own zone of defence covered, but Campese kept running out of their zones, one after another. Finally, only John Kirwan was left, and he allowed Campese to turn him around. I suppose this was a mistake by Kirwan, but it did not matter anyway, because Campese had Phil Kearns and Rob Egerton in support, each of whom would otherwise have scored. Nevertheless, the fact Campese ended up scoring *outside* Kirwan was remarkable.

There is a small story behind this try. Against Argentina three weeks earlier, Campese had set up a try after running at a similar angle quite unintentionally. John Eales had thrown an awful pass, which Campese gathered only with difficulty. At this point, he found that the only direction left for him to run was across the face of the Argentinian defence. A hole appeared in the defence, Campese went through it and Tim Horan

David Campese demonstrates his brilliance early in the World Cup semi-final, bamboozling the All Black defence by running on a slanting angle to score a classic try.   Photosport

scored under the posts. This gave me the idea of using this method of attack again if an opportunity presented itself. So at training afterwards I tried to get Campese to practise running at the slanting angle, but he found it difficult to do. All his instincts were to close the angle and run straight. Eventually, I decided to show him myself how easy it was. So, with ball in hand, I ran across the field while Campese watched. He applauded derisively when I had finished, but he had obviously not missed the point.

Five minutes before half-time, despite our dominance of the play, we led by only 7 points. We had been playing with the wind, so 7 points was hardly enough. Happily, we scored a second try just before half-time, so we led 13-nil at the break, which I thought was probably enough to win. The players must have thought so, too, because they went into their shell in the second half. We defended well, but we had lost the aggressive drive we had had in the first half. In my experience, Australian teams have a tendency to do this — in fact, we did it again in the final against England — and it is a tendency we must try to get out of our system.

The try Australia scored towards the end of the first half was replayed endlessly on television and, I predict, will be shown again and again in years to come. It was Lynagh, running towards the blind side, who set things in motion. Noticing that the New Zealand backs were lined up flat, he chipped the ball into the gap behind the winger. The New Zealand fullback, Kieran Crowley, was regarded by the Australians as being a little

Nick Farr-Jones probes the blind against the All Blacks in Dublin. Photosport

slow off the mark, and no doubt Lynagh had this in mind when he chose to kick in front of him. Campese was bearing down on the ball, and I think Crowley was undecided whether to go in for the ball or wait for the bounce and try to stop Campese. His slight hesitation gave Campese the fraction of a second he needed to scoop up the ball and flash past him. Campese's running then was superb. He drew two defenders and had a third one chasing him, all of whom thought he was a threat. Campese saw Tim Horan behind him out of the corner of his eye and flipped the ball back over his shoulder. Horan did well to catch it before going on to score.

The score at the end was 16 to 6. It was a great win and in a state of some exuberance I hurried to the dressing room to congratulate the players. It was an L-shaped room, and I immediately went around the corner of the L to speak to the players there. I told them in a loud voice: 'There was only one team out there. You absolutely killed 'em. The score flattered them.' I was still saying this as I walked back around the corner — and found the New Zealand coach, Grizz Wyllie, standing inside the door of the dressing room, congratulating a few of the Australians. I was most embarrassed. Wyllie had been generous enough to come in almost as soon as the game was over to congratulate us, and the last thing I wanted to do was offend him. I apologised to him, saying I did not intend him to hear what I had just said. He replied, 'Don't worry about it. You were right, anyway. There was only one team on the field.'

On the day after the match, a Sunday, we packed up at the Westbury Hotel in Dublin, where we had been staying, and headed out to the airport to catch a plane back to London. By chance, we came face to face with the New Zealand team at Dublin's airport terminal. They were sitting there waiting for their plane to Cardiff. They were obviously very downcast, but they wished us luck and one or two of them said, 'Whatever you do, don't let England beat you.' There was not a trace of ill feeling towards us, who were the cause of their misfortune. The New Zealanders are not accustomed to being losers in Rugby, but in my experience they are good losers, nevertheless.

A famous moment for the Wallabies: The final whistle at Lansdowne Road with the All Blacks defeated. Next stop, Twickenham.   *Allsport*

21

CHAMPIONS OF THE WORLD

O ne of the first matters I had to deal with on becoming national coach again in 1988 was the choice of the the Australian team's captain. During the previous year, Andrew Slack had retired after four years as captain, and Simon Poidevin had been appointed to lead the team on its tour of Argentina late in the year. In my deliberations on the matter, a number of factors presented themselves. One was that I felt Simon's own form throughout 1987 had not been up to the high standard usually expected of him. In view of this, I could not be sure he would be an automatic choice for the coming Tests in 1988. I am strongly of the view that the captain has to earn his place in the side as a player. His selection should never be influenced by the fact that he is needed for his captaincy. I therefore decided to look past Simon for someone whose form ensured he would be a first-choice selection for the team and whose personal qualities fitted him for the captaincy. I decided to recommend Nick Farr-Jones.

It was an unusual choice in one respect: Nick had not captained a representative team before. In fact, as far as I know, he had not captained any kind of team since leaving school. However, I felt this inexperience was more than compensated for by the respect and admiration which other players had for him as a player and as an individual. This proved correct. Farr-Jones soon mastered the job. He set high personal standards for himself, and because of his maturity and strength of character he was able to set high standards for the team quite naturally and easily. He understood from the outset when and how the team needed to concentrate and when and how it needed to relax. His influence on the team in all its activities on and off the field has been vital to its success. Without it, I am sure we would not have won the World Cup.

As a player, Farr-Jones is supreme in his field. Unhesitatingly, I rate him the best scrum half in the world today. He has the advantage of being an exceptional athlete. He was a schoolboy middle-distance champion, and he is very fast over short distances, too. In a series of repetition sprints in New Zealand in 1990, Nick consistently led Ian Williams over the distance, which I think was thirty metres. Australia has always had good halfbacks, but until Farr-Jones came to the fore we had not had a *great* halfback for some time. For this reason, I believe Farr-Jones gave the side another dimension. He possesses a unique ability to orchestrate the team on the field — that is, to see the picture, assess the situation and spit out instructions. All through a match he shouts directions — 'Cover the right. Go out, go out. Move it up there. Break, break. Get off, get off.' His presence in the team in the semi-final against New Zealand had been crucial, in my opinion, and our physiotherapist, Greg Craig, has my eternal gratitude for helping Nick make it on the field. Now that we were going into the final against England, I knew Nick's presence would be crucial again.

England qualified to meet us in the final of the World Cup by defeating Scotland in the other semi-final in what I considered a poor game of Rugby. To judge from its performance in that match, the England team had little concept of mid-field play. They had three superb mid-field players in Rob Andrew, Will Carling and Jeremy Guscott, but as a unit they were largely ineffective — a point I have made elsewhere. They rarely played in such a way as to provide space and opportunities for each other and for the other backs, most notably the winger Rory Underwood, who is an exceptionally dangerous ball-runner.

On the other hand, I had enormous respect for the England forward pack, which I consider fit to be compared with any forward pack of any era. The very fact England had this great strength in its forwards clearly influenced it to play the type of game it had been playing in the previous few years. Australia had a great forward pack, too, which had succeeded in resisting England's attempt at domination through the forwards in the Test in Australia earlier in 1991. Wade Dooley had been absent from the England team in Australia, and we knew his return for the World Cup would make a difference. I regard Dooley as one of the world's great second-rowers, a player who individually is capable of influencing a game.

Most commentators, including the Rugby writers on the London newspapers, were predicting an Australian win. We were confident, too, yet we knew that the Englishmen would be a much tougher proposition at Twickenham than they had been in Australia four months earlier. This time they would be playing in-season, not out of season as they did in Australia. Another important factor was that they would be playing on their home turf in front of their own supporters. Realising this, we went to some lengths to try to turn the disadvantage of playing at Twickenham into an advantage. We had discussion sessions and did mental rehearsals to plant the idea firmly in the subconscious minds of the players that the cheering for England at Twickenham was actually a motivational spur for us.

On our return from Dublin we stayed at the hotel outside London where the All Blacks had been staying a few weeks before, a comfortable establishment in Surrey with a nine-hole golf course attached. It was private and sedate, a place where we could get away from everyone except the media. The hotel appeared to be constantly overrun by journalists. They came from all parts of the British Isles, from France, Italy, New Zealand, Argentina and, of course, from Australia. It was impossible to walk through the hotel without someone wanting to take you aside for an interview, and this was despite the fact we had set up procedures whereby the media could obtain interviews in an orderly way. The pressure of this media attention seemed to grow exponentially, day by day, the closer we approached the final.

On Thursday, two days before the final, we cut off the media's access to individual players, and on that same day we had our last practice session behind closed doors. We did make an exception for one media person, the Rugby broadcaster Bill McLaren, who had not been able to get down to London earlier. He needed to familiarise himself with the Australian players so he could identify them when describing the match on radio. McLaren watched us train and told me later that what he had seen was consistent with everything he had heard about the Wallabies — namely, that they possessed exceptional ball-handling skills. After one ball-handling drill, he said to me, 'Ask your boys to do it a little slower next time — I couldn't even see the ball.' We already knew we were admired for these ball-handling drills, for the spectators at earlier training sessions had sometimes burst into spontaneous applause. Naturally, this encouraged us to do those drills all the more.

The prelude to the World Cup final at Twickenham was an ordeal for the players. They were out on the field for an inordinately long time before the kick-off while both teams were introduced to the Queen and other dignitaries and the anthems were played. We did not start the match at all well, and I am sure this was one reason. The crowd, naturally enough, was largely on the side of England, but we did have an unexpectedly strong contingent of supporters. Among them were the Scotland players, who, I was told later, had turned up at the match wearing not only their own Scottish uniforms but green and gold Australian scarves and caps. Thus attired, they walked through the carpark at Twickenham and were loudly hooted by the England supporters there.

We expected the Englishmen to try and attack through our mid-field as they had done with limited success in Sydney earlier in the year. They had made a few holes in our defence then and we thought they were bound to try it again. We were so sure of this, in fact, that we spent some time analysing the deficiencies of our defence in that area. The main threat would come from their spare forwards running between their five-eighth and inside-centre and between their two centres. We worked out ways to

The Queen meets the star of the show, David Campese, before kick-off in the 1991 World Cup final at Twickenham. Skipper Nick Farr-Jones looks as though he has his mind on the rugby ahead. Photosport

counter this, even to the point of nominating which of our defenders would be responsible for which attacker. The strategy paid off. The Englishmen did try the tactic again, but this time they did not make any holes.

We also paid a lot of attention to scrummaging. Our loose-head prop, Tony Daly, took the precaution of cutting the left sleeve of his jersey, knowing that the English tight-head prop, Jeff Probyn, made a practice of pulling down on his opponent's sleeve while scrummaging. This is an illegal practice, of course, and I find it astonishing that Probyn has been scrummaging illegally like this for as long as anyone can remember without ever being penalised for it. In the World Cup, three loose-head props that I know of, Steve McDowell of New Zealand, David Sole of Scotland and Tony Daly of Australia, cut the left sleeves off their jerseys before going out to mark Probyn. The players take it for granted that Probyn does it, radio and television broadcasters often speak about it, the whole Rugby world knows about it, yet somehow the referees remain blind to it. Even if by some freak of nature a referee was unable to see Probyn doing this in scrum after scrum, the touch judge on that side is supposed to report it.

We won the match 12 to 6. The Australian players themselves believed they had not played at their best and certainly not as well as against the All Blacks a week before. We started the game far too tentatively and were on the back foot for the first ten minutes. Neverthe-

Australia produced better rugby in 1991 than in the World Cup grand final against England, but there was no more important victory. Here Nick Farr-Jones services his backline protected by Ewen McKenzie.   Photosport

less, we had much the better of the first half and with an ounce of luck might have had a decisive lead at half-time. We were deprived of one try when a ball which Campese chipped ahead after making a break down the right wing bounced backwards and touched the referee, who consequently had to call a scrum. In fact, the match produced only one try, and this was scored by Tony Daly. Tim Horan had chipped ahead in a marvellous counter-attack from his own 22, and Campese had chased the ball and forced a lineout in the corner. For what I think was the only time in the tournament, Rod McCall called Willie Ofahengaue at number five. Ofahengaue went up and took a two-handed catch, and the try was scored from there. The key to the whole exercise was Horan's grubber kick. If it had gone into touch, England would have had the put-in. Instead, it went down the line but stayed in play, forcing Jonathon Webb to run the ball into touch. It was another instance of how the outcome of a match can sometimes turn on the single bounce of a ball.

One of my memories of the first half is of Simon Poidevin retaining possession after he was brought down in a heavy tackle by Micky Skinner. The tackle shook the bones of the people watching from the grandstand, so I can imagine its effect on Poidevin. After the match, I asked Poidevin in a light-hearted way how he enjoyed the tackle. He replied, 'I didn't lose possession, did I?' That was the important thing.

Having led by 9 to 0 at half-time, we started the second half with a

Above: Tony Daly, who was to score the only try in the World Cup grand final, prepares to grapple with big Wade Dooley following a lineout. Below: Marty Roebuck is grabbed from behind, but look at the support, from Tony Daly, Rod McCall, Phil Kearns and Ewen McKenzie.   Photosport

surge. Willie Ofahengaue charged up the field, brushing aside defender after defender. Nothing came of this, however, and then England began to assert control. Thereafter, we fought a rear-guard action, and for some time England attacked our line relentlessly, giving us a number of anxious moments. One reason for our slump in the second half was that almost every time we won a lineout the referee penalised us. It was rumoured there had been some discussion between the touch judge and the referee at half-time, as a result of which the referee came down heavily on us — most unfairly, in our view.

There was one area of play where England had certainly had the better of us in the second half of this match, especially from the lineouts, and this was first-phase possession. England's second-rowers, Wade Dooley and Paul Ackford, with assistance at the back of the lineout, were largely responsible for this. As a result, Australia was hard-pressed to hold England out in the last twenty minutes or so of the match.

I have two strong memories of this period of play. One is of the continuing failure of the England mid-field to provide the space England needed to go over the line, although to be fair to the England mid-field it must be said that Australia had a very well-organised, disciplined and capable defence. In this respect, I consider our centres, Tim Horan and Jason Little, to be without peer in world Rugby. In fact, they are the best defensive pairing I have ever seen in the centres. The England team had obviously gone into this match believing it had to do something extra — that it could not hope to beat Australia if it played as it did in its pool matches. They had apparently concluded (as we had concluded) that this type of game presented too few tactical options to threaten the Australian defence. Their solution was to launch an all-out attack with the ball in hand, something which surprised us and delighted the crowd. Ironically, the fact that they still failed to breach our defence with this more expansive game helped us compensate for our lack of first-phase possession by enabling us to gain more second-phase possession. This was because the pressure of our defence frequently forced England to turn the ball over.

My other memory of this period of play is of a number of fine individual performances in defence. I remember an outstanding tackle in cover defence by Nick Farr-Jones on Jeremy Guscott. Guscott is a player of speed, yet somehow, in a moment of desperation, Farr-Jones pulled him in. I remember John Eales' seemingly miraculous tackle on Rob Andrew when the try-line looked completely open. This tackle followed an unfortunate decision by the Australian backs to run the ball when the backline consisted only of Marty Roebuck, who had moved into five-eighth, Michael Lynagh at inside-centre and David Campese outside him. I was looking for the ball to be kicked into row 10 of the northern stand, and to my dismay the ball moved across our depleted backline. Lynagh, having looped Campese well behind the advantage line, lost possession in a

So that's how world champions unwind . . . in the bath. Michael Lynagh, Simon Poidevin and Phil Kearns enjoy a big soak before starting their World Cup celebrations after defeating England.   Photosport

tackle, and the England players set off for the try-line. Somehow, Eales managed to perform his extraordinary feat of cover defence.

I have since seen it suggested by some people in the England camp that if England had not changed its tactics it may have won. But each game is an entity. You cannot change one part of it and assume the rest would have been the same. If England had played its normal game, the entire balance of the match would have been different. For instance, it was the pressure put on the Australian defence by England's expansive game which forced us to put the ball into touch so often and so give England so much first-phase possession. If they had not played the expansive game, things would probably have been very different.

The cause of the biggest controversy in the match was the referee's ruling after David Campese's arm bunted the ball forward as it was being passed by Peter Winterbottom to the England winger Rory Underwood, who at that stage may have had an overlap. The referee ruled it a deliberate knock-on and awarded England a penalty. The England hooker, Brian Moore, thought the referee should have awarded a penalty try. I took the opposite view. I thought it was harsh of the referee even to award a penalty. He could easily have ruled that the ball was simply passed into Campese's extended arm and that Campese made no deliberate attempt to hit it. In any case, Moore did get his arithmetic wrong. He suggested that if England had been awarded a penalty try it would have drawn level with Australia at 12-all and might have gone on from there to win. This is not correct. In doing this sum, Moore counted the 3 points England actually earned from the penalty kick whereas, of course, there would have been no penalty kick if the referee had awarded a penalty try instead. In other words, Australia would still have been ahead by 12-9, and I see no good reason to believe that England would have improved on that.

A moment to treasure forever. Nick Farr-Jones and player of the tournament David Campese hold the Webb Ellis Trophy aloft at Twickenham, appropriately framing Australian Rugby president, Joe French. Photosport

We did not play at our best, but we were still the better side on the day. We won playing a different kind of game, but in my opinion that was one of our strengths. We were a team for all seasons — we could win in a number of ways.

Nick Farr-Jones told me several times later that he thought the game against England was a lot harder than the game against New Zealand. I am not sure whether this was a fact or merely his impression. I have already described how the pressure of the tournament had begun to take its toll on Nick by the time Australia went into the final, so his impressions of the match against England may well have been influenced by his own condition. My own view is the New Zealand match and the England match were about as tough as each other.

An abiding memory for me at the end of the match was the unrestrained joy of the non-playing members of our squad, players such as Anthony Herbert and Jeff Miller. Miller, I remember, was over the moon with delight. These reserve players had been a strength in the touring side from first to last. Two of them, David Knox and Richard Tombs, did not play at all, and another six or so played only one match. Yet their general support and enthusiasm and, in particular, their great efforts at training had a real bearing on the performance of the team. We invariably trained as a squad of twenty-six, so they were always part of the enterprise. At the end, they were at least as happy about the outcome as the fifteen who came off the field.

IN THE OLD COUNTRY

R ugby teams from the British Isles do not always play great Rugby, and too often they have played bad and boring Rugby, but nearly always they play Rugby with character. As a teenager, I knew all about the great British and Irish players of the day, men such as Tony O'Reilly, Peter Jackson, Lewis Jones, Jackie Kyle, Cliff Morgan. I read about them avidly and studied photographs of them in action. Perhaps because they were all so far away, I viewed them then with a sense of wonder, which I have not lost entirely even today. Perhaps this is why the prospect of coaching an Australian team in the British Isles will always have for me a special appeal.

In recent years, England has been the most dynamic force in northern hemisphere Rugby. I find this interesting, because it is the result of a deliberate effort by English authorities to raise standards at the top level. In 1988 England sent a team to Australia for a series which we won two Tests to nil, and we did it playing badly. Shortly after that tour, English authorities decided the time had come to rule a line beneath their last defeat and make a fresh start with a new set of policies. In particular, they set out as a matter of urgency to raise the England team's standards of preparation to the level already existing in the two leading southern hemisphere countries, New Zealand and Australia. By the time the World Cup came around in 1991, they had managed to do this. In my view, the best-prepared teams in the World Cup were Australia and England. The next-best prepared teams, I thought, were possibly Canada and New Zealand.

Other British Isles teams have not been so successful, although it is hard to blame them for that. Indeed, the consistently high quality of the teams fielded by Scotland and Ireland is, in my view, one of the marvels of the Rugby world. How these two countries keep discovering so many good players in such a relatively small playing population is astonishing. Not many Australians or New Zealanders appreciate the fact that Rugby in Scotland is confined largely to a string of border towns like Hawick and Melrose and Selkirk, most of which are no bigger than, say, Goulburn or Gympie. Yet the standard of Rugby played in these towns is exceptionally high. For the most part, these are rural towns and, if I am not mistaken, a sizeable proportion of the men playing Rugby there are from surrounding farms, which may explain why they make such rugged opponents on the field. Europe's agricultural policy may be unpopular with Australian farmers, but if it is enabling those stalwart men of the Borders to go on playing Rugby then there is something to be said for it.

Ireland is different. As I saw it, Rugby is mainly a middle-class, white-collar game there, more or less as it is in Australia, which means that Irish teams are liable to be under-prepared. This is how I have found them — talented, certainly, but under-prepared. They have enough spirit and flair to be able occasionally to pull a great performance out of the hat, but no team can have a continuity of good performances if the players are not strong and fit. Perhaps because my grandfather, Matthew Dwyer, came from Ireland, I feel a natural attraction to what I see as Ireland's distinc-tively Irish approach to the game. Irish Rugby players are tough, belligerent and passionate. They are capable of rising to impressive heights, and unfortunately they have made a practice of rising to these heights whenever they play Australia. Australian teams touring the British Isles have invariably found Ireland the hardest nation to beat, regardless of how Ireland may have been faring against its neighbours. There is no better example of this than our narrow escape at Dublin in the 1991 World Cup.

Andrew Slack once spent the off-season playing in Ireland, and I happened to speak to him on his return. I asked, 'How was it?' and he replied, 'Fantastic.' I said, 'You mean the Rugby was fantastic?' He replied, 'No. The Rugby was awful.' He proceeded to tell me he did not know what misery was until he played outside-centre in Ireland and stood for eighty minutes on a cold, muddy pitch, waiting for a ball which never arrived. It was the fun off the field, shared in the company of delightful people, he said, which made Rugby there so enjoyable. I agree. The Irish are delightful. They also make very talented Rugby players. All the great Lions teams over the years have been fortified by Irishmen. It is is hard to think of more talented five-eighths than Ollie Campbell and Mike Gibson or a more talented centre than David Hewitt. They have had great forwards, too, Willie John McBride among them. In 1991-92 I rated the Irish front row, in particular, as being of the highest quality.

No amount of talent, courage and determination can compensate for poor preparation, however. Quite apart from how it affects a player's performance on the day, a lack of physical preparation ensures he will take longer to recover from the match. I get the feeling the Irish find it hard to keep backing up with good performances, which is usually a sign that a team is unfit or inexperienced, or both. Ireland's problem, as I view it, is

Willie John McBride . . . one of the great Irish and British Lions forwards.
Peter Bush

a lack of fitness. I think it is a pity that Ireland teams aren't prepared better. Someone once said to me that the Irish play Rugby merely for the fun of it, as if this were an excuse for not being fit. The reality is there is no conflict at all between enjoying Rugby and being fit. They ought to be two sides of one coin. If Rugby authorities in Ireland were to concentrate on improving the preparation of their players, not merely by fine-tuning existing programs but by instituting new, scientifically based programs, as we did and the English did, I have no doubt that all the other Five Nations teams would find Ireland as hard to deal with as we Australians always have.

Scotland was Australia's opponent in my first Test as coach in 1982, and ever since Rugby teams wearing Scottish colours have had a special significance for me. In my experience then and since, the outstanding feature of Scottish Rugby has been forward play. The Melrose coach Jim Telfer is acknowledged as being responsible for this. Telfer toured New Zealand several times as a player and then as a coach, and it seems he was impressed by the hard, low, driving forward play he encountered there, which he concluded was a key to the New Zealanders' success. My guess is that Telfer decided that the same kind of the low, driving ruck would not only suit playing conditions in Scotland but would suit the natural disposition of Scottish forwards. There is, after all, a lot that is Scottish in New Zealanders. Thus, the great Scottish forwards I have seen since I first became national coach have been forwards right out of the New Zealand mould — tough, no-nonsense players like John Jeffrey and Derek White.

Jim Telfer . . . used New Zealand techniques to improve Scottish forward play.

Mike Brett

I should point out that I do not equate no-nonsense play with dirty play, although there has been one Scottish forward of recent years, Finlay Calder, who seemed intent on getting away with as much as he could. Footballers often resort to this kind of play to compensate for the fact they are getting old and slow, and this may be the explanation in Calder's case.

I said before that Scotland has made the most of its relatively small Rugby resources. Its shortage of numbers inevitably shows up, though, in an inconsistency in the size of its forwards. The Scots may field an occasional big forward, but often they go into matches with second-rowers who are much too small, and they also tend to lack big, strong front-rowers. Scottish forwards are certainly tough and willing, but in international Rugby size is itself an important factor. If the big forwards aren't there to choose, however, the Scottish selectors cannot choose them. Thus, you find that some of Scotland's finest front-rowers have been players who might have been ruled out as too small in other teams, men such as Ian McLauchlan and David Sole. Both have been great players — strong, tough and skilful — but both would have been greater still if nature had endowed them with a little more size and weight.

Gavin Hastings was one Scottish player I held in very high regard, so much so that I always included him in my world XV. In the World Cup semi-final against England in 1991, however, Hastings took an option which showed how pressure can cloud the judgment of even the best players. I said as much to Scotland's coach, Ian McGeechan, when we were at a dinner together afterwards. The situation was that Scotland had to score in the dying moments of the match to win. Hastings took the ball somewhere near his own line, perhaps even in his own in-goal area, and ran it up. He got through the first line of defence, a marvellous feat, and was running with support when the cover defence closed on him. What did Hastings do? He kicked the ball. I thought at the time: 'Oh, no! And I picked you in my world XV!"

Kicking the ball was the one thing Hastings could not afford to do under the circumstances. His team's only hope was to keep the ball in hand. At worst, the Scots were assured of the scrum feed if one of them had been tackled. As I have said elsewhere, I consider it bad Rugby to be dependent on the other side making a mistake. Hastings' attitude should have been: "We desperately need to score, but we can only score a try if we have the ball, and to score I need to control the play." Still, Hastings is a player of high quality, who may yet find his way back into my world XV.

I might add that Hastings' brother Scott is, in my view, one of the great defenders in international Rugby. I am not suggesting he is a bone-crushing tackler, but he is extremely capable at reading attacks and knowing what has to be done, and where to do it, in defence. Without him, I don't think the British Lions would have beaten Australia in 1989.

There has been a lot of discussion lately about Wales' decline as a

Gavin Hastings, left, a quality player who's always in my world XVs, and, right, his brother Scott, who is one of the great defenders in international rugby.

Mike Brett

Rugby power. So many people have come up with theories about it that I am sure the Welsh themselves are by now entirely confused. As someone viewing the problem from afar, I hesitate to add my voice to the chorus, yet the health of Welsh Rugby is a matter which concerns me and to which I have given some thought, and I do have an opinion about it. My view is that Welsh Rugby has been too insular — that the Welsh have been too concerned with how their players were performing against each other internally at the club level. It seems to me they have been measuring their strength by how Cardiff fared against Pontypool or how Pontypool fared against Swansea. If Cardiff, or Pontypool or whatever club did well, the Welsh were happy. They had lost sight of the big picture.

I make the point elsewhere that Rugby in Wales, as in New Zealand, always had the advantage of being a people's game — a game played by men of all classes and occupations — which meant that Welsh teams had a core of physically tough manual workers. I am not overstating the importance of this. Before Australia and other countries started running intensive physical preparation programs, the Welsh and the New Zealanders had a significant natural advantage in physical toughness whenever they ran onto a Test field. The gymnasium has become the great leveller. Australians are able now to develop the degree of strength and toughness in the gym which the Welsh and New Zealanders traditionally have developed by their lifestyles.

The Welsh have been an inspiration to the rest of the Rugby world for as long as the game has been played, and I am sure the rest of the Rugby world would love to see Welsh Rugby rise again. Australia should never again be able to crush Wales by 63 to 6, as it did in Australia in 1991, for that result did more discredit to Wales than it did credit to Australia. The source of all those brilliant Welsh players over the years must not be allowed to dry up. I am thinking of players of the class and brilliance of Cliff Morgan, Barry John, Gareth Edwards, JPR Williams, Gerald Davies, Bleddyn Williams. Rugby League has made serious inroads into Welsh Rugby and, as in Australia, League tends to buy up the great midfield players whose loss is felt keenly afterwards. Jonathan Davies is one such loss of recent years. I am confident this problem will eventually be solved by the progressive relaxation of Rugby's amateur rules. Cynics might say that these rules are already lax in Wales, but even if this were true the Rugby players there can be earning only peanuts, and peanuts will not dissuade a player from accepting a £100,000 offer to switch to League.

Finally, we come to England, the number-one power of European Rugby in recent years. Unlike the Scots, the English have enormous depth in Rugby. I became aware of this when I toured England and Wales with the Randwick team in 1973. I was astonished at how many good players there were in England, and ever since I have understood why it has been a perennial problem for the English to choose just fifteen from the mass of good players available. This isn't such a bad problem for a country to have, of course. One of my main objectives in Australia since regaining the national coaching job has been to increase the number of players at the top level by bringing through new players able to challenge for representative team positions.

English Rugby has taken what seems to be a turn for the better. Previously, England teams played safe Rugby. They would never fight a battle they thought they might lose, by which I mean they would never risk defeat to achieve victory. My attitude is different. Risking defeat to achieve victory in Rugby has always seemed to me a most honourable endeavour. Instead, the English played Rugby as if each match were a war of attrition. Provided they took no risks and were able to deny the opposition any easy chances, they counted on the superiority of their play prevailing in the end. The trouble was that against teams like New Zealand and Australia their superiority, if it existed at all, was insufficient to produce the victories they desired. For year after year, whenever they came south to play these countries, England took a beating. Its wars of attrition were not being won, so clearly they had to do something more.

Even after they found themselves with an extremely talented side in 1988 and set about improving the team's preparation, the English clung to their old error-free ideal. The English mind seemed to think like this: 'We need to get the ball in front of our forwards to allow them to batter the opposition into submission, and the best way to get it there without incurring a risk is to have it kicked, either by Richard Hill the scrum half or Rob Andrew the five-eighth. Alternatively, we can use our powerful forward pack to smash its way through the opposition and maybe then, if belatedly, we might use the skills of our backs.' One pity about this approach was that the skills of the English backs were unsurpassed. No team in the world in recent years has had a backline with better skills than Andrew, Carling, Guscott and Underwood. Not to make full use of them was, in my view, not only a waste, but it seriously limited the scope England had to place its opponents under stress.

I felt while watching the 1992 Five Nations matches that England had finally come round to the idea that it needed to expand its game beyond

Jeremy Guscott . . . a vital part of a wonderfully skilled international backline. Only recently has England started to use it.   Allsport

this highly controlled, error-free, lets-kick-it-and-hope-the-opposition-will-make-a-mistake approach. Instead, the message I read in the England play was: 'We're a really top side. We're capable of threatening the opposition in many more places on the field than we have been. If we can pressure the opposition in midfield in particular we're going to multiply our chances of scoring.' This is what the English did, and I thought they played very well. Their 1992 team was, in my opinion, markedly better than the side we beat in the final of the 1991 World Cup, which raises the hypothetical question: Would Australia have beaten England's 1992 team? I feel sure we could have, because I do not believe Australia played well in that World Cup final. An Englishman would argue, no doubt, that England prevented Australia playing well, but I cannot believe we would not win a lot more ball if the match were replayed tomorrow.

English Rugby is extremely well off. It is strong in playing numbers and strong in financial support. It also has very capable administrators, who at times may seem absurdly conservative yet whose ability to organise and run tournaments is outstanding. One of their wisest moves in the past twenty years was to make use of the talent and toughness of Rugby players in the north of England, who previously had been on the outer. More recently, their wisest move was to establish programs under which top players would be properly and comprehensively prepared. Such a system appears to have been in place since 1988, and the results are there for all to see. English Rugby has one advantage which I envy as an Australian — the geographical compactness of the country. Because distances are small, squads can be assembled with a speed and ease which would be impossible in Australia or even in New Zealand.

Although I spoke admiringly before of the more open style of Rugby being played by England, I still think the most important difference about English Rugby today is that its players are fitter and physically harder, thanks to the preparation programs I discussed before. England players have always possessed discipline and technique. Now, because they are fit and physically tough, they can maintain the discipline and technique throughout the match. It is fatigue, more than anything, which causes a team to lose its discipline and technique.

The excellent technique of the English is a characteristic of Rugby players in the British Isles. Whatever else you may say of them, they do tend to be technically correct. Their close-quarter play in scrums, lineouts, rucks and mauls, in particular, is extremely sound. At Randwick over the years we have had a number of visiting players from Britain and Ireland. Some were in the twilight of their playing careers and understandably were a little ponderous. Even the younger players were generally not as fit, fast and aggressive as we might have liked. But you could always rely on these players from Britain to possess excellent technique. It is one of British Rugby's finest traditions.

23

THE MIGHTY ALL BLACKS

Lately, Australians have had a good deal of success against their old rivals the All Blacks. Our victory over them in the World Cup semi-final in 1991 meant we had won three of the last four encounters, a cause of deep satisfaction among Australian Rugby followers. Australians would be wise to keep things in perspective, however. Over the years the All Blacks have had much the better of their contests with us. By the end of 1991 they had won sixty-four Tests against Australia and lost only twenty-four. Even over the past thirteen or fourteen years, a period in which Australia has certainly closed the gap on New Zealand, the All Blacks have managed to win more Tests against us than they have lost. We may have won a few recent battles, but the All Blacks are still winning the war.

The lesson of history is clear: New Zealand has been an immensely and consistently powerful Rugby nation. Indeed, I find it hard to think of another country which has performed so well over such a long period in any international sport. How and why New Zealand has managed to dominate the game has intrigued me ever since I started taking a deep interest in Rugby after leaving school. In those years there was an Australian player at Randwick named Ted Heinrich, who was, by our standards, an extremely tough, fit and determined flanker. I recall talking to him after he had played against New Zealand in some match or other and hearing him speak with amazement of the hardness of the New Zealand players. 'It's unbelieveable — those fellas are like concrete,' he said. 'I hit them with my hardest tackle and I bounce off.'

This kind of talk, which was fairly common among Australians at the time, did nothing for the confidence of players who had to turn out against the All Blacks on the field. I know that as a young player I regarded New Zealand players with some awe, and I am sure I would have been typical in this respect. I suppose, in retrospect, they deserved to be regarded with some awe, but we were wrong to think that in some intrinsic way they were supermen. There was nothing special about Rugby players from New Zealand. They were simply prepared better than their Australian opponents. That was the difference.

All the New Zealand teams I have seen have been very good and some have been great. Choosing which was the greatest is not easy. In the ten years since I first coached an Australian team against them, I would probably nominate the All Blacks of 1987-88 as the strongest, although I do think that the All Blacks of 1982 were also very strong. The 1982 side did have one big plus in my view — its captain, Graham Mourie, who was a marvellous strategist. But I think the side of 1987-88 was fitter and more powerful. Its magnificent record is a measure of its quality.

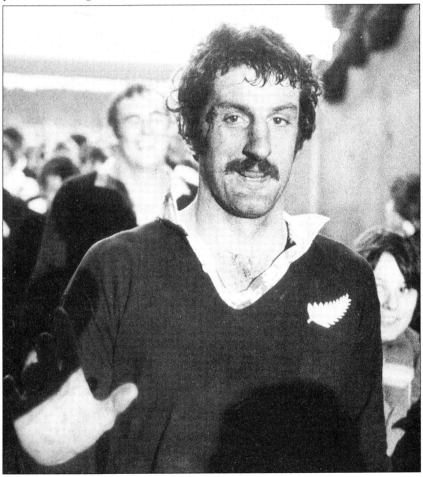

New Zealand's captain against the 1982 Wallabies, Graham Mourie . . . a wonderful strategist.   Colorsport

Grizz Wyllie was the coach of that All Black team. His team was great, and I suppose many people would say Wyllie was a great coach, too. His record suggests that he was. This is why I was not unhappy when New Zealand decided to appoint John Hart as 'co-coach' of the All Blacks for the 1991 World Cup. I knew it would be a plus for Australia's chances. It was rumoured that Hart and Wyllie did not get on too well and, moreover, that Hart was after Wyllie's job. Offering them joint responsibility for the team was, in my opinion, a ridiculous decision. From conversations we have had since, I gather even Hart thought it was ridiculous. It was rather like the Australian Rugby Union appointing Alan Jones as my co-coach. I felt at the time that if I had been Wyllie I would have resigned, but I realise it is easier to say this than to do it. I had nothing at all against Hart, but I sympathised with Wyllie. I respected him as an individual, as I had respected him as a most formidable player. How he looks is how he played. I have no views, either way, on how effective he was as a coach, because I simply have no way of knowing. His record, I repeat, is a good enough testimony.

John Hart . . . appointing him as co-coach to the World Cup with Alex Wyllie was as ridiculous as suggesting Alan Jones and I share the coaching of the Wallabies. Norman Smith

Over the years it became clear to me that New Zealand Rugby Union players and Australian Rugby League players had a lot in common. They both played an extremely hard, aggressive, physical-contact type of game, and they did it week after week. I was particularly struck by this on our tour of New Zealand in 1990. As always, the provincial teams there played the hard, physical, confrontation-style game I referred to before, but this time there was something else about their game which reminded me of Rugby League in Australia. Several provincial teams had adopted the League-type approach of trying to smash through the opposition defences. For two or three tackles they would try to crash through close-in, just as they do in League, and then perhaps put a kick up. I saw big, heavy centres lining back deep and accelerating on to the ball with the aim of smashing through the opposition, like forwards in League running one and two off a play-the-ball. It was a classic Rugby League method, and I considered it a retrograde development in Rugby.

I suggested before that the preparation of Rugby players in New Zealand has been a key to their success. Of this I have no doubt. The All Blacks who ran out on the Test field had all been playing this hard physical game, week after week, year after year. Their opponents, whether Australian or English or French, had probably experienced this kind of play only rarely, so they found it difficult to cope with. Over the past fifteen years or so, Australians have played New Zealand much more regularly, and they have become used to the New Zealand style of play. We have come to realise, as New Zealanders have always realised, that players must be hard and fit. I use the term 'hard' here in a physical sense. Rugby players at the international level need to be low in body fat and high in muscle bulk. If you poke a finger into the body of an international Rugby player, you should find it hard and resistant. This is probably what Ted Heinrich had in mind thirty years ago when he told me the All Blacks were like concrete.

This is not the only reason for the All Blacks' success, of course. Tactically, their great strength has been their play at the breakdowns, and for this, I am told, they owe a great deal to the Otago coach of the late 1940s, Vic Cavanagh, whom I have heard referred to as the 'father of the ruck'. (I find it interesting that in 1992, in their hour of need, the New Zealanders have turned to another Otago coach, Laurie Mains.) For some reason, New Zealanders have always been viewed in Australia as footballers who did not play with the ball in hand and therefore were not to be admired. The truth is the All Blacks play more with the ball in hand than any team I know. The difference is that they play a smashing game with the ball in hand, not a dashing one. Essentially, the All Blacks' strategy, which I gather was developed with Otago by Cavanagh, is to try to get the ball in front of the advantage line by carrying it there aggressively. The forwards then set out to smash their opponents backwards and throw their retreating defences into disarray and, having done that, to use the ball again, perhaps wider this time. This type of game is dependent on the forwards arriving very quickly at the breakdowns, which, of course, is how the All Blacks operate.

Another great feature of the All Blacks' play is their ability to apply pressure at their opponents' most vulnerable point. They are very quick to identify a weakness in their opposition, and thereafter they will attack that weakness remorsely. It's rather like a crack in the dam wall. The pressure becomes more and more intense until the dam bursts. This is what the All Blacks do — they burst through the crack in the opposition's defences with an enormous surge of manpower. My recollection of this goes back to Fred Allen's great All Black teams of the 1960s. I can see in my memory a black avalanche descending on some hapless player, and at the front of the avalanche is Waka Nathan, the 'black panther'. Conversely, the All Blacks are more adept at hiding and protecting their own weaknesses than any team I know. Often we have identified a New Zealand player we considered not quite up to to standard, but invariably, supported by his team-mates, he has played well. Kieran Crowley is a good example. We have looked at Crowley and agreed among ourselves that he was a little on the slow side and that we should be able to take advantage of this, but invariably he has come out and played a fine game. In fact, I believe he played an important part in New Zealand's two victories against us in 1990.

There are sociological factors, too. Rugby in New Zealand has always been a people's game in the sense that it is played by people of all social strata, which meant their teams were filled with men who worked in hard, manual jobs — farmers, meatworkers, labourers and so on. The same is true of Wales and, to some extent, South Africa. In Australia and most other Rugby countries, Rugby has been played mainly by middle-class men in white-collar jobs, who without question were physically softer. Unfortunately for New Zealand, this natural advantage is rapidly being eliminated. The movement of people to the cities has gradually changed the make-up of New Zealand teams. Nowadays, they are as city-based as Australian teams. What is more important is that other Rugby nations today put so much emphasis on physical preparation that the players they put on the field against New Zealand are increasingly as hard and fit as the New Zealanders.

Australian Rugby players have improved their preparation enormously since the 1970s. The New Zealand example has been one reason. Another has been the saturation exposure of Rugby League on television, which has shown Rugby Union players in Australia what a high degree of fitness and toughness can and should be achieved. A third influence has been the rise of Queensland Rugby over the past twenty years or so. In their determination to get the better of New South Wales, Queenslanders have made big improvements in their preparation. For all these reasons, I believe that

The All Blacks perform their haka, something I consider to be a ridiculous practice.

Rugby players in Australia, at least at the representative level, are now as well prepared as the All Blacks.

Someone asked me recently if I ever gave Australian players instructions on how to react to the Maori haka which the New Zealanders perform before each Test. My reply was that I could not recall ever having raised the matter with the team, for the simple reason I did not see it as being of any importance. I could not care whether my players stared at them or ignored them, or whether they stood in front of them or walked away. I do have strong views, however, on the question of whether the haka should be performed at all. Frankly, I think it is a ridiculous practice. For one thing, there are usually few players in the New Zealand Test side who are Maori. In my view, it is just as silly for players like Grant Fox, John Kirwan and Sean Fitzpatrick to be out there doing the haka as it would be for players like Michael Lynagh, David Campese and Nick Farr-Jones to be doing an Aboriginal corroboree.

My chief objection to the haka, however, is that it is an unfair distraction to the other team. By all means, let the New Zealanders do the haka before a Test. After all, it provides some entertainment for the crowd, rather like the floorshows the Rugby League people put on before big matches in Australia. But they should do the haka before the other team is brought on the field. It is wrong and plainly unfair that one team should have its concentration distracted because the other team is allowed to perform a ritual which has nothing whatever to do with the game. The minutes before the kick-off are extremely important for players trying to prepare themselves mentally for the match. By doing the haka the New Zealanders can maintain their focus, but their opponents are left with a lack of focus. It is no defence to say the haka is traditional, that New Zealanders having been doing it for as long as anyone can remember. Many other traditions have disappeared because they were judged for whatever reason not to be worth keeping. Rugby teams used to line up before a match and shake hands with each other, but you never hear anyone complaining that this tradition has gone. The tradition of the haka ought to go, too.

In recent years, the All Blacks have played open and attractive Rugby. Around the world they still have a reputation for playing dour Rugby, but it is a reputation they no longer deserve. The biggest improvement in New Zealand Rugby over the past six or seven years has certainly been in backline play, and I think the Australian influence has had a lot to do with this. The improvement has been under way for probably ten years, but it is over the past five years that it has become particularly evident. In the third Test of the 1986 series against Australia, New Zealand ran the ball wide with enthusiasm and commitment. In the following year, the arrival of John Gallagher from Britain added enormously to the performance of the New Zealand backline. Moreover, Grant Fox's ability to use the ball accurately gave people like John Schuster, Joe Stanley, Gallagher and the two outstanding finishers, John Kirwan and Terry Wright, plenty of room to move.

When we were in New Zealand in 1982 and enjoying unexpected success with a team of raw recruits, the New Zealand director of coaching, Bill Freeman, approached me one day and said he would like to have a chat

Bill Freeman, then coaching co-ordinator of the New Zealand Rugby Union, with whom I spent a fruitful afternoon exchanging 'secrets' back in 1982.

Peter Bush

about our backline play. I agreed, and we set aside an afternoon to meet in his office at Wellington. He began by saying, 'Look, I can see what your people do. What I can't work out is how you actually practise it and get them to do it. It isn't easy to line up close and flat and run straight at

John Gallagher, whose introduction to the All Blacks helped the development of their back play.   *Peter Bush*

opposition defences. It's fraught with danger, and players tend to shy away from danger.' I replied, 'Bill, I'm prepared to discuss that, provided you're prepared to discuss your play at the breakdowns. You tell me some of your secrets about this, and I'll tell you some of my secrets about that.' So we agreed to do a trade, and spent a long afternoon exchanging information, which was a productive exercise for both of us.

By 1986, the All Blacks had started to run the ball much more, but they were still not doing it well. In 1987, they straightened up their attack noticeably. It seemed to me they were intent on getting full value from the several good running players they possessed, most notably John Gallagher. They realised that their mid-field needed to become more constructive to make space for the players out wide and, significantly, they dropped the five-eighth Frano Botica, who was essentially an achieving player rather than a constructing player. It is interesting to note, incidentally, that Rugby League teams have since chosen to play Botica on the wing, where he can achieve as much as he likes without having to worry about construction (or destruction) in mid-field. In place of Botica, the selectors brought in Grant Fox, who, despite his faults, is good at choosing the options, particularly which side of the field to run. The faults I see in Fox's game are in positional play, although these have largely been compensated for by having players of quality such as John Schuster and Joe Stanley outside him. Even though Fox may have been a little out of position, Shuster's speed enabled him to adjust that positional play before the ball moved too wide.

Although New Zealanders have generally had the better of the contests with Australia over the years, Australians were able repeatedly to pop up with an occasional great performance and beat them. Australia won many times like this when it was patently the inferior team, which, as I know, was a cause of some vexation among Rugby people in New Zealand. This, I like to think, is consistent with the Australian national character. Australians have traditionally had an irreverent attitude to their superiors, and New Zealanders had long been their superiors on the Rugby field.

Times have changed. Today, New Zealand can no longer count on being superior. An Australian victory over New Zealand is no longer an upset win — it is a win by a better team. The New Zealanders, I believe, are themselves very conscious of this new state of affairs. At the return Test in Auckland in 1991, I sensed for the first time that this was a New Zealand team nervous and apprehensive about the outcome. When they won 6-3 and so saved the Bledisloe Cup, it seemed to me they were not so much jubilant as relieved, which confirmed my earlier impression. The All Blacks will no doubt win many Tests against the Wallabies in the years ahead, but I predict that those victories will become harder and harder to achieve.

THE BALL IN HAND: FURTHER REFLECTIONS

I attended a Rugby night in Sydney recently at which Andrew Slack, who captained the Wallabies on their grand slam tour of Britain in 1984, spoke about the tour and showed a video of some of the matches. One piece of film showed Slack in his usual outside-centre position straightening his attack and going right through the defence and beyond the advantage line before meeting the cover defence. The Australian forwards capitalised on this, the ball was moved to the blind side, and Australia scored a try. When I saw this on the screen I called out to Slack, 'Running straight, I see.' He called back, 'What else could I do? All I heard from you in 1983 was run straight, run straight.' This was true. I had hammered the idea into him repeatedly because, like many other players, he had trouble running straight. I kept telling him he wasn't running straight, and he kept insisting, 'Bob, I must be running straight. I'm trying to run straight and I feel I'm running straight.' To convince him, I made a special arrangement with the ABC to run a tape off its head-on camera at Ballymore. I showed Slack the tape afterwards, and he was able to see for himself that he was not running completely straight, as I wanted him to.

Running straight is difficult. This is one point I am prepared to concede to all the critics of my backline play. It is no more difficult, however, than winning a match against a tough opposition. When I tell players to run straight I mean it literally — they must run parallel with the touch lines. On the other hand, I do not say that they must run straight *all* the time. Someone who did not agree with the idea of running straight once said to me, as if to score a point against me, 'How can you run straight if you're going to do a scissors pass?' Obviously, there are many occasions like this where you cannot run straight. My point is that when you think you're running straight, make sure this is what you are doing.

I began introducing my type of backline play to the Randwick team in 1977, but it was only in 1978 that the team began using with it with much authority. We then had an intriguing situation in Sydney Rugby. At one end of the spectrum, we had the Randwick concept of backline play as taught by me, which I had inherited from Cyril Towers. At the other end, we had the Brockhoff concept of Rugby, as taught by Dave Brockhoff, Australian coach in the 1970s. The Brockhoff approach, basically, was to try to keep the ball in front of the forward pack by kicking it there, the idea being that the forwards would then drive in low and hard over the ball, smashing the opposition out of the way. Brockhoff was said to have picked up the concept from Ted Jessup, who coached Eastern Suburbs when Brockhoff played for the club, and in turn Jessup was said to have acquired it from a fellow New Zealander, Vic Cavanagh, who, as I said earlier, won a great reputation coaching Otago in the late 1940s. The characteristic of Cavanagh's game was a low, driving ruck which smashed the opposition backwards and released good ball.

Thus we had two Rugby philosophies, poles apart, one of which could be traced to Cyril Towers and the other to Vic Cavanagh. About this time, however, I was lent a copy of an audio-tape interview Cavanagh had done many years before. As I listened to the tape I could have sworn that it was Cyril Towers talking, because the views Cavanagh was expressing were identical with Cyril's. Cavanagh's strategy was to get the ball in front of the forward pack to enable the forwards to smash the opposition in the ruck and release good ball to the backs, who would then take the ball over the advantage line by aggressively attacking the opposition's defences with the ball in hand. This was precisely what Cyril Towers had advocated, and precisely what I was coaching at Randwick. Somewhere between Cavanagh and Brockhoff the concept had gone off at a tangent. Instead of taking the ball over the advantage line by hand, as Cavanagh recommended, the idea now was to get it there by kicking. Cavanagh, I feel sure, would have disowned it.

Before I took over the coaching job at Randwick in 1977, Randwick had never won more than three Sydney premierships in a row. Since 1977 Randwick has not once failed to make the grand final. I sometimes speak to people from other clubs who admit this is a marvellous record but say, 'Yes, but you get all the best players.' This is not true. I usually invite these people to examine our top players, one by one. I say to them, 'How about Ewen McKenzie? Was he a superstar when he came to Randwick,? He walked into training one day and nobody knew who he was. Was Phil Kearns a big catch when he joined us? He'd played second-fifteen Rugby at school. Or how about Lloyd Walker? He played second grade for Randwick for five years before anyone had heard of him, either.' And so the list goes on. I agree that David Campese and Simon Poidevin were rather valuable recruits, but these two players were exceptions who hardly ever play for Randwick — and who would deny that their play has been improved by their time at Randwick?

Vic Cavanagh, the great Otago coach of the 1940s. His coaching strategies are still influential in Australia today.

The flat backline alignment offers an important advantage for forwards, too. There is nothing a big forward likes less than having to run back to cover a mistake by the backs twenty metres behind the advantage line. He does not mind, though, having to cover a mistake three metres *in front* of the advantage line.

I spoke elsewhere of how an attacking backline should aim to engage the entire defence, man on man, and so maintain the advantage in numbers it started out with. If it manages to do this and still has an extra man, the only way the defence can prevent a break is by some last-moment adjustment. In other words, a defender will need to read the play correctly, work out where the ball is going and tackle the player trying to make the break. This is where the need for pressure comes in. If you can put the defenders under pressure and give them less time to adjust, they will obviously be much less likely to make the right adjustment. The more you can hurry and fluster them, the better your chances of getting through. By doing this, you are working on the defence not only physically but mentally.

So the twin aims must be to engage all the defenders, one by one, and put them under so much stress that they will not be able to adjust. How do you do this? This brings us back to the first principle underlying the strategy — namely, that you cannot put the defence under pressure until you are under pressure yourself. I regard this as elemental. A team can play non-pressure Rugby all day if it wishes to, but it will not achieve anything by doing so. You cannot push a needle through a cloth until you get the needle very close to it. This is why we stand flat — that is, closer to the defence.

Some people have wrongly assumed that it is part of my plan to get players to throw the ball in foolhardy fashion about the field, as if they were the Harlem Globetrotters. There is nothing foolhardy about the type of play I advocate. On the contrary. My type of play is more structured than any other type of play I know. Indeed, if it does have a fault it is that it's overly structured.

We had three outstanding mid-field players in the World Cup team, Michael Lynagh, Tim Horan and Jason Little, but I could not say they were an outstanding mid-field. They have the potential to be, and I hope before long they will be. I regard Lynagh as one of the great players of international Rugby for at least a generation. I first saw him on Coogee Oval when he was practising for, I think, the Australian under-17 team. I asked the coach Jeff Sayle: 'Who's that little blond-headed kid over there?' Sayle replied, 'Don't knock him — he's the star.' I assured Sayle I was not knocking him. I was immediately impressed by him.

I rate Lynagh the equal of Mark Ella in general play and his superior in kicking. I would love to have an opportunity to influence Lynagh's positional play, running angles, tactical options and other areas of his play on a day-to-day basis over a whole season of club Rugby. He is a marvellous player, yet I believe he has not achieved his full potential. I rate him Ella's equal in general play because of his ability to break the line of defence. He has a wonderful side-step at full pace, which has invariably proved successful when he has chosen to use it. He did use it to break New Zealand's first line of defence on one memorable occasion in the semi-final of the 1991 World Cup. He carried the ball many metres over the advantage line, thereby setting up David Campese's try.

One advantage Mark Ella had over Michael Lynagh is that he was constantly under the influence of people who were well-versed in the type of game I advocate. If Michael were to enjoy this same advantage, I feel sure he would make as big an impact as a running player as Mark did. One of Mark's great gifts was his eye for an opportunity a couple of passes away. Mark could smell a try. Michael possesses the same gift, if not to the same extent as Mark.

Tim Horan is already a great player, although he, too, has not yet realised his potential. He is not a good passer of the ball, and I do not believe so talented a player should be in any way deficient in such a basic skill. He is an extremely strong runner, possessing both balance and speed, and he has great physical courage, which he demonstrates in his tackling. I often think he must make a difficult opponent, being so fast and so aggressive. I expressed the opinion to someone recently that if you could put Lloyd Walker's head on Tim Horan's body you would have a superchampion. Horan is young enough to have time to develop a brain like Walker's.

Jason Little may be even a little faster than Horan. I believe Horan himself thinks this is so. Little is a natural athlete. He is tall and, contrary to the impression some people gain from television, quite powerfully built. He was a champion high-jumper at school and he certainly has the highest vertical jump of all the Australian players. Little has always struck me as

Tim Horan - in action here during the World Cup match against Argentina - is a great player but not yet a great passer of the ball.   Photosport

being an outside-centre on classic lines. He is tall, fast, lithe and long-striding. I rate him perhaps the best defensive player, technically, in the world.

If I had to condense my Rugby philosophy into one sentence, I would repeat a statement I made in an earlier chapter, namely that I want to keep the winning of the game in our hands and not put the onus on the opposition to avoid losing it. Primarily, this means pressuring the opposition into mistakes with the ball in hand, rather than giving the ball to the opposition and then trying to pressure them into mistakes. If we have the ball in hand, we own the game. If we give the opposition the ball by kicking it, we are effectively giving them ownership of the game. When I was coaching Randwick in the late 1970s I became irritated by comments in the press suggesting that Randwick was vulnerable to a side which kicked well. Our next match was against Parramatta, which played the kicking game, mainly through its five-eighth, Tony Melrose. Out of sheer perversity, I told Mark Ella before the match that whenever he got the ball that day I wanted him to kick it behind either the blind or the open winger. He asked why, and I said, 'Because I want to show these dopey bastards that it's really an easy thing to do — that you don't have to be anything special to win that way. I want to show them that we can win that way if we want to.'

Ella did as I told him to. After the match Parramatta's coach, Peter Fenton, told me that he had just seen Ella kick more in one game that Melrose did in three games. We proved our point. Randwick won comfortably. We could have won that way every week. The reason we did not try to is that we saw there was a better, more challenging, way to play the game. The distinctive thing about Rugby which makes people want to play the game is that you can run with the ball in hand. To spend the afternoon kicking and chasing it, it seems to me, defeats the purpose of playing it in the first place. You might as well play soccer or Australian Rules. Randwick once played a seven-a-side match against a team which I knew had won matches by kicking. Before the game I told John Flett, 'This mob are going to kick the ball against us a lot today. I want you to hang back as fullback and when you get it and the opposition are coming through after it I want you to kick it back to the other end of the field and you chase it.' This is what Flett did, and by the end of the match he almost needed treatment for exhaustion, but we won by about 25 points. I told our players, 'See, it isn't hard. Don't ever think it's a big deal to win that way. When another team does it, feel sorry for them, because they don't have the confidence to try something else.'

I have said many times that one of the main reasons Australian Rugby has been stronger over the past fifteen years is that Queensland Rugby has been stronger. Anyone needing to be convinced about this should look at Queensland's recent record against New South Wales. Both states take these annual interstate fixtures very seriously, and rightly so, yet we should not let ourselves become preoccupied with them. The danger, as I see it, is that we will be misled into thinking all is well if New South Wales is beating Queensland impressively, or if Queensland is beating New South Wales impressively, without regard to how each of them might be rating

Tony Melrose . . . used by Parramatta to pursue a kicking game.

on the international scale. By focusing too much attention and energy on the interstate matches, we put a limit on our wider aspirations. If the main goal we set ourselves is simply being good enough to beat Queensland, or good enough to beat New South Wales, we risk falling short of the standard we need to meet if we are to win at the international level. This very kind of insularity, I believe, is one of the reasons for Wales' decline as a Rugby power.

The problem can manifest itself in a number of ways. Here is one example of what can happen. The New South Wales selectors choose a player who is specially equipped to do what they consider needs to be done to beat Queensland. Yet this player, perhaps because of physical inadequacies or a deficiency in talent, may have no hope of ever making an impact at the international level. This is why Australian selectors have for some years now been digging 'beneath' the New South Wales and Queensland teams to find new players for the Test side. Some of our best players today were plucked out of relative obscurity in this way — Daly, Kearns, McKenzie, Ofahengaue, Gavin, Nasser, Horan, Little. With the exception of Daly, all these went straight into the Australian team from New South Wales or Queensland B teams. Daly had not even made the New South Wales B team. At the time he was chosen to play for Australia he had played no representative Rugby at all since his under-21 days.

I saw Jason Little play for a Brisbane team against London Irish in 1988 and was immediately impressed. In the following year, 1989, I watched Little and Tim Horan play for the Queensland B team. Their potential was obvious, and having seen them the other selectors and I decided we should not merely choose from players in the A teams. Accordingly, Little and Horan were picked for the tour of France later that year. On the other hand, we often see someone playing well at the interstate level who, we decide, is nevertheless playing to the limit of his ability and would be unable to take the next step up. Judgments of this kind are never easy to make, but selectors are obliged to make them.

It is a pity that Rugby writers often do not give the selectors credit for this. They will point to a player who has been excelling in interstate matches and castigate the Australian selectors for being stupid enough or negligent enough to overlook him. If any player has been excelling in interstate matches, I can guarantee that we will have studied him very, very closely. Within the past year or two, we selectors were taken to task severely by the Sydney press for ignoring the claims of a certain New South Wales player. We were accused of being blind to the player's obvious Test potential. The truth was I could have sat any of those writers down beside me and shown them videos of various matches in which this player made several critical mistakes which, in my view, showed clearly his limitations. An opposite example is Willie Ofahengaue. The higher the level of competition, the better he plays.

25

MONEY AND THE GAME

I t has long been obvious to me that a steady and irreversible move towards professionalism is under way in Rugby. This move, I believe, is gathering so much force that we can now confidently expect to see international Rugby players being paid to play the game, probably before this decade is over. The only uncertainty is how the payments will be made. They may be in the form of straightforward match fees or they may be in the form of contributions to a trust fund which is released to players on retirement. Either way, the end result will be the same. Already, Rugby's laws have been relaxed to allow players to earn money off the field by endorsing products, writing books, making personal appearances and the like. The Rugby administrators who agreed to these changes probably thought they were making big concessions. In fact, they were merely giving the first inch. Sooner or later they will have to give a mile.

On today's market, a top Rugby player ought to be worth at least $A100,000 a year — or, say, £50,000 a year in Britain. By giving endorsements and making personal appearances, they would stand to earn much more than this. I do not consider $A100,000 a year a generous return for their skill and effort, merely a reasonable one. Cricket serves as a model in this regard. The top cricketers — those who play Tests and one-day internationals — do earn excellent money, much more than men of their age could ordinarily hope to earn in any other way. The cricketers on the level below them, such as Sheffield Shield cricketers in Australia, might not earn a great living from the game but they are reasonably well rewarded for the time they spend on the field. Below this level, at the club level, the game is almost entirely amateur. There are said to be about 550,000 registered cricketers in Australia. If you do the calculation you find that fewer than 0.01 per cent of them are full-time professionals and about 0.02 per cent are part-time professionals. In other words, at least 99.97 per cent of cricketers in Australia are amateurs.

This is about the extent of the professionalism I would expect to see in

Rugby. Even if you paid the top players well, you would still have a game which was almost entirely amateur. I know a great many Rugby people would not be persuaded by this. They would argue that if you pollute the top level of the game with professionalism the pollution will seep right through. I can understand their fears, and I certainly believe that Rugby administrators should proceed with care when they begin introducing professionalism to the game, as inevitably they must. Rugby's adherence to the amateur ideal over the years has not been the only reason for the special spirit which exists in the sport — and which, in my opinion, exists in no other sport — but it has certainly been an important reason. Administrators must take pains to ensure that this unique Rugby spirit is treasured, that it is not put at risk by the advent of professionalism. It need not be.

The truth is that the community's conception of amateurism has changed enormously over the years. The sportsperson who abided by the amateur code at the turn of the century would be viewed as a fanatic today. In those days a player could not call himself an amateur if he allowed his sport to pay his medical bills after an injury on the field. He was even expected to pay for the bandages that were put on him in the dressing room! As recently as 1946, when England players resumed their careers after World War II, they were told by officials to make sure, when they arrived to play in the Test match, that they brought along the socks they were issued in 1939, since the uniform was still the same. International players at that time were still buying their own shorts. Not even diehard traditionalists would say now that top Rugby players should buy their own shorts. They would not dream of calling Nick Farr-Jones a professional because he is issued with four tracksuits, four jerseys, ten pairs of shorts and three pairs of boots at the start of the season.

My point is that the ideal of amateurism is not a static thing. It has changed with the times. This is why, if we go about things the right way, I am sure we can pay our top players yet still maintain the game's amateur ethic and so preserve Rugby's special culture. Far from harming Rugby, I have no doubt it will benefit the game. It will certainly lift Rugby's profile. By the time this book is published, the Australian players are likely to have been contracted to the sports management company International Management Group. We may be certain that IMG, simply by advancing the interests of the players, will automatically achieve greater exposure for the game.

Paying the top players will also ensure they stay in the game. This is particularly important in Australia, Wales and, to a lesser extent, New Zealand, countries where there has been a steady leakage of players to Rugby League. I have never known a Rugby player to switch to League because he thought it a better game. Some may have been seeking another challenge, but I would suggest that in every case money was the primary attraction. Mark Ella did not leave Rugby to play League, of course, but I wonder whether he, too, might not have stayed, despite his dissatisfaction with the game at the time, if there had been a financial incentive for doing so.

During a conversation about all this the other day I was asked by a well-meaning Rugby person whether I wasn't at all concerned about the consequences of paying leading Rugby players to play. I replied that of course I was concerned. How could anyone who loved Rugby and cherished Rugby's culture not be concerned? Obviously, there are risks. In my opinion, however, the risks must be taken for the good of the game, and if we proceed with care the risks can be made negligible. For instance, Rugby administrators must frame the laws controlling payments to players to ensure that the game itself is not deprived — that there is still enough money to develop the sport among juniors. Rugby must also be careful to avoid the situation in which players are paid more than the game can afford. Rugby League in Australia has saddled itself with this problem by paying League footballers more money than the game generates at the turnstiles. The players' income has to be heavily subsidised by gambling money from poker machines — an unnatural situation which I believe is inherently wrong. In League, of course, the number of professionals runs into the hundreds. In Rugby Union, the number would run into only dozens.

Golf is a good example of what we ought to be aiming at. At the top level, the sport is awash with money. The big-name golf pros, I believe, earn more money than people in almost any other sport. Yet this has not affected the essential culture of golf as it exists at courses all over the world. The ethics of golf, its code of behaviour, the spirit of the game — all these have remained intact in spite of the money. American Football provides another example we could follow. It is a highly professional sport, yet it has been extremely protective of its image. Any player, no matter how prominent, can count on being dealt with severely if he does anything to bring the game into disrepute.

I find it curious that the Rugby people who oppose the idea of paying leading players, who profess to be aghast at the very thought of it, do not seem to mind in the slightest if other people in Rugby are paid. This is one of the great ironies in the issue. So far as I can see, everyone in Rugby is paid except the players, the coach and the referee, who, of course, are the very people responsible for attracting paying customers through the turnstiles. While I was in Britain for the World Cup in 1991, I discussed the idea of paying players with a Rugby official from another country, who was horrified at the prospect of it and told me how it would threaten the fabric of the game. I asked him, 'But don't you get paid by the game?' He admitted he did get paid but insisted this was a different matter entirely. It wasn't a different matter. I pointed out to him that the people doing his particular job in Rugby were not always paid. They used to do it for nothing. The players, I said, still did it for nothing. If he was now on the payroll, why shouldn't the players be on the payroll, too? It was, I think, a fair question.

In recent years there has been an ever-increasing number of people in Rugby who get paid. Not long ago I attended a meeting of Rugby officials in Sydney. There were fourteen of us at the table and only three were not on the Rugby payroll — myself, my assistant coach, Bob Templeton, and the president of the Australian Rugby Union, Joe French, who is a retired man anyway. In certain other countries, all fourteen of us may have been paid. In the British Isles, stories abound about coaches who are provided with sham jobs but who, in reality, are being paid to coach. This, I can say with certainty, is something that has not happened in Australia.

I can also say with certainty that players in Australia are not paid to play. Whether or not this is true in other countries I do not know. We all have heard the stories of players being paid in Wales and Italy and France. According to rumour, England is another country where the practice is not uncommon. There is a widespread belief in Australia that it is common for players in England to receive quite generous compensation at the club level. Ironically, it seems to be widely believed in England that the same thing happens in Australia and New Zealand. This is definitely not true, so perhaps the rumours we hear about England are not true, either. I do admit that in Australia you hear from time to time of players receiving financial compensation in the form of rent-free accommodation or inflated payments for the petrol they use driving to and from training. There is a joke told of a player who was receiving so much petrol money that someone asked: 'What does he travel in — a Boeing jet?' I do not know if these stories are true, but I do know that the players they are told about are not players at the top level. In any case, the sums involved could only be trifling.

Even if these stories about rent-free accommodation and petrol money were true, it would be reasonable to ask this question: What on earth is the difference between receiving rent-free accommodation and earning money from product endorsements? For that matter, what is the difference between earning money from endorsements and being paid a match fee? The principle is the same in every case — the player is simply recompensed for his time and skill. It is absurd, it seems to me, for one to be legal and the others not.

In 1983 the Australian Rugby Union called a meeting of interested parties to discuss demands by players. The players wanted a better deal in a number of areas, including the daily allowance permitted to players on tour. They argued, correctly, that $A20 a day was simply not enough to pay for essentials such as toothpaste, shaving cream, phone calls and the like. During the meeting someone circulated a paper which sounded, on first

*Probably I'm pondering the vexed matter of professionalism in rugby. I
believe we can expect to see international players being paid before the
decade is over.*   John Fairfax Group

reading, as if it had been written the day before. As we learned later, it had
actually been written at the turn of the century, when Rugby's hardline
position on amateurism was fostering a good deal of discontent among
players, which led a few years later to the creation of Rugby League in
Australia. Obviously, time had worked few changes in official Rugby
thinking. In 1983 the game was facing the same kind of threat it faced
eighty years before, and the threat was just as serious. Rugby officials
ignored the threat then and paid a heavy price. The lesson for us at the
meeting was not to ignore the threat again.

My greatest fear is that national Rugby bodies around the world will
seek to close off the few avenues for making money which the International
Rugby Board has already opened up for players. The problem I can see
arising is that players will be prevented from endorsing products which are
in competition with products endorsed by their Rugby administration.
The players will be told they can endorse anything so long as it isn't a car,
or a football, or a beer, or a football boot or a line of leisure clothing,
because the Rugby administration has given endorsements for all of those.
The Rugby players will then be entitled to ask, 'What is left?' I have warned
about this in Australia. I have told several administrators that if they do
this, if they tell the players they can make money in theory while in
practice there isn't any money for them to make, they will provoke a
justifiable rebellion. Rugby administrators must accept the intent of the
new laws on amateurism, not just the letter of those laws. In the words of
W.E. Gladstone, 'You cannot fight against the future. Time is on our side.'

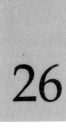

RUGBY LEAGUE'S
UNCERTAIN FUTURE

Rugby Union and Rugby League have been living together in Australia for a long time now in what might be termed a peaceful co-existence. One is an amateur game and the other a professional game, and for years neither has made much ground at the expense of the other. For the most part, each has generally been content with its own portion of the sports market. It is a situation which, I suppose, would ordinarily be expected to continue indefinitely. There are changes under way in Rugby, however, which may cause the boundary between the two codes to be redrawn. I refer in particular to Rugby's irreversible move towards professionalism, which, I predict, will have far-reaching consequences for League. For the first time in over eighty years, I believe League in Australia is about to feel a sharp edge of competition from the code it broke away from so long ago.

Let me at this point state clearly my attitude to Rugby League. I regard the men who play it as fine athletes, and I regard its administrators as outstanding. The professional expertise with which they have managed, promoted and marketed League has given a lead to all other sports in Australia, including Rugby Union. On the other hand, I consider the game itself to be repetitive. I see a number of things wrong with League as a game, and by far the most serious of them is that its laws have devalued teamwork. By teamwork, I simply mean the scope a player has to construct an advantage for a team-mate. I consider teamwork to be not only one of the great skills of the Rugby game but also one of its great pleasures. I assess players according to their ability in this regard. If I see a player who can move defences around and use support players, I rate him a good player. If he cannot do these things, he isn't, according to my definition, a 'good Rugby player'.

Two things determine how a game is played — one, the laws of the game and, two, the structure of play built around those laws, usually by coaches. Frankly, I consider the structure of play in League to be predictable and monotonous. I believe the game is unworthy of the talented men who play it. League not only has players of great talent but it has them in depth, and I envy League for that. I could not count the number of times Rugby people from other countries have said to me that if Australia's two Rugby codes ever combine Australia will be unbeatable. I sometimes watch League players on television and think to myself what successful Rugby Union players some of them would make. I am sure Martin Bella, for instance, would be a most effective Rugby prop. He has the strength and build for scrummaging, and also the pace and ability to run with the ball. Bradley Clyde, I think, would make an outstanding open-side flanker. He is not such a big man, but he has great pace and running ability and is a most decisive tackler. Paul Sironen would certainly do well in Rugby as a back-row forward, for he has both height and speed. Ian Roberts would probably do well in the same position.

Of the backs, Steve Ella comes immediately to mind as a player who would have been outstanding in Rugby. I thought he was a marvellous support player, who possessed continuity skills and that special 'vision' which enables a player to play a team game. I have no doubt Steve Ella would have shone more brightly in Rugby than in League, where, I think, his worth was never fully appreciated. I can imagine Eric Grothe being extremely useful playing right wing on the short side of the scrum, and Wally Lewis would probably have made a successful Rugby player, too. If Lewis played Rugby the way he plays League he would not have excelled, but he is such a good player I am sure he would have been able to adapt his game to suit the other code. Lewis is above all a powerful player — a powerful runner and a powerful tackler — a fact which League commentators seemed to overlook. Mal Meninga would surely have made an impact in Rugby, probably at inside-centre, where he would have been more than useful in getting the ball past the advantage line.

As a general rule, I have found that League players tend to be excellent catchers of the ball but poor passers of the ball, the simple reason for this being that catching is viewed as important in League and passing not so important. Most League players possess exceptional fitness and most have good speed. Some lack balance, some lack good handling skills and many lack handling subtlety. Handling subtlety is not, I admit, a requirement of League as it is played today, yet I consider its neglect a great pity. It was not always neglected. There were big, strong League players in the past — Duncan Hall senior is one who comes to mind — who possessed subtle handling skills of a kind not seen in League today.

By contrast, Rugby demands a huge range of skills, all of which must be possessed by every player at the top level. I once had an interesting conversation on this subject with Terry Fearnley, a prominent League coach in Sydney, who later took on the job of coaching the Southern Districts Rugby Union team. I met Fearnley at a coaching accreditation course. He said to me: 'I cannot believe there are so many things to learn about this game. There are just so many facets to it, especially in the forwards. I never realised coaching it would be so hard.' In fact, Fearnley did not ever come to terms with coaching Rugby. He had been an outstanding coach in League, but his lack of background in Union told against him, and eventually he gave it up.

The range of skills and the subtlety of skills required in Rugby set it apart from League. This emphasis on skills does have a disadvantage. If Rugby is not played well, if it is not played with a fairly high degree of skill, it can become ragged. I agree entirely with those League people who complain that Rugby is not nearly so attractive to watch when it is not played at the top level. The explanation is that because Rugby demands a higher degree of skill it is a harder game to master, and because it is a harder game to master it is more liable to be played badly. There is much more impromptu play in Rugby than in League, and much more stereotyped play in League than in Rugby.

Above all, Rugby is an enjoyable game to play. After thirty years of mixing with footballers of all kinds I have yet to meet anyone who has played both Rugby codes and did not consider Rugby Union the more enjoyable game to play. Apart from anything else, Rugby compels players to adjust more and think more about the game; it makes a greater demand on its players mentally than League does. I concede that League is a more physical game, but I question whether this sole fact ought to be counted in its favour. Running into brick walls is physical, too, and nobody should enjoy doing that.

If Rugby is a superior game and a more enjoyable game, why then has League been the more popular game in Australia for seventy years at least? The basic answer to this question is that a big proportion of any population will always prefer the simple to the complicated. Many more people listen to pop music than to classical music, for instance, which does not mean that pop music is better. So we find that soccer, which is about the most simple football game in the world, also has the world's biggest following. There are hardly any rules in soccer for spectators to think about, and they can see the ball all of the time. Rugby Union has many rules, and for half the time the spectators cannot see the ball. Rugby League has fewer rules, and spectators can see the ball most of the time. League is, by comparison with Rugby, a simple game. Every time a League player is tackled, the ball becomes dead and play has to be re-started by a play-the-ball. I know this all takes place in a matter of seconds, but nevertheless it determines the tempo of the game, which is stop-start, stop-start, stop-start. The pattern of play this produces is so repetitive and uncomplicated that anyone can follow it.

Rugby's appeal is much more complex. In Rugby, the aim is to establish a continuity of advantage, and by its very nature this requires subtle and intricate skills. To understand and appreciate these skills is one of the joys of the game. We all know from experience that the more complicated a thing is and the harder it is to master, the greater the satisfaction we experience once we do manage to master it. This is true of Rugby. It is also

Wally Lewis . . . starred in league and would probably have succeeded in rugby, too.

the reason, incidentally, that Rugby followers are among the most fanatical of all sports followers.

Not long ago I was quoted in a Sydney newspaper predicting the demise of Rugby League. This probably seemed to most readers a rather far-fetched prediction to make, given that League in Australia is more popular today than ever before. In fact, I was merely speculating what might happen in the not-so-distant future when top Rugby players start to earn as much as top League players. Such a situation is, I think, a fascinating one to contemplate. Until now, the movement of players has been all one way, from Rugby to League. When Rugby starts paying its top players as much as League, I predict the movement will be almost entirely the other way.

If you could represent Australia in a genuinely international sport, go on regular tours to a dozen or more countries around the world *and* be paid for doing it, why would you want to stay in the restricted world of Rugby League? It is reasonable to imagine a situation in which Rugby will constantly cream off some of the best League players, those who have a good chance of playing Rugby for Australia. All this is speculation, of course, and things may not turn out just as I have suggested. What I can predict with certainty, however, is that the coming professionalism in Rugby is destined to cause League a few problems.

Instead of competing with each other, could the two codes somehow meet each other half-way and amalgamate? Perhaps, but I am inclined to think not. Rugby is a world sport, after all. It is inconceivable that the International Rugby Board, which represents more than a hundred countries, would agree to amend the laws of the game to accommodate Rugby League in three or four countries. On the other hand, I do think that, whereas the two codes have been gradually moving apart for most of this century, it is possible they may start to move together again. We already have seen both codes moving together to increase the reward for scoring tries. Rugby Union moved up to the four-point try, then League moved up to the four-point try. Rugby Union has now moved up to a five-point try, and it may be that League will follow it again. All these changes have been made in recognition of the fact that tries are what spectators really come to see. So there has been some meeting of the minds by the two codes on this matter, and I am sure, given the right encouragement, that there could be much more.

Ultimately, the self-interest of the players themselves must prevail. This is what encourages me to believe that sooner or later the present barrier between the codes will be broken down. Consider this simple hypothesis. Up to a certain point in history, Rugby League did not exist. What brought it into existence was discontent among Rugby players over financial matters. If the grounds for that discontent cease to exist, the need for two codes should also cease to exist. That is the logic of it. Let us wait to see what happens.

THE RETURN OF THE SPRINGBOKS

No matter what else happens, the most exciting event in international Rugby in the 1990s is destined to be the return of South Africa to world competition. We have not seen the Springboks in Australia for twenty years and more, but we have certainly not forgotten the power and energy with which they play the game. After all these years the Springboks still have a daunting reputation in Australia and, I daresay, in every other Rugby country. In my own mind they loom at least as large as the All Blacks. Most Rugby followers of mature years will remember the Springbok prop, Andy McDonald, who was said to have fought off a lion with his bare hands. The story may have been exaggerated, but it seemed consistent with everything we had come to know about South African forwards. The image Australians had of them was of huge men who played the game with a fierce single-mindedness. The image we had of their backs was of big, strong men who ran with speed and aggression. Together, forwards and backs, they presented a potent combination.

We will find out soon whether the Springboks are as good as Australians remember them. Not long after this book appears in print, the Wallabies are scheduled to play one Test in South Africa. Naturally, I have some reservations about going there. Other things being equal, it would be wrong of us to risk our reputation in a one-off, winner-takes-all contest, especially on opposition territory. We will have everything to lose and hardly anything to gain. But other things are not equal. A number of our senior players such as Nick Farr-Jones, David Campese, Michael Lynagh and Simon Poidevin will be retired before an Australian tour of South Africa is slotted into the regular international schedule of matches. The opportunity to play in South Africa in 1992 is the first and last these players will ever get, so they are all eager to grasp it while they can. It was for the sake of these players, who have given wonderful service to Australian Rugby over many years, that we decided to accept South Africa's invitation to play the single Test there. It is a gamble, but one worth taking.

Like the Australian players themselves, I eagerly await this first encounter between the South Africans and the Wallabies and, personally, I feel quietly confident about the outcome. I know for sure that Australia is a far more powerful Rugby nation than when the two countries last played each other. On the other hand, there is no reason to believe the Springboks are any stronger now than they were then. If anything, after their long isolation, you would expect them to be weaker. Historically, Australia has a passably good record against the South Africans, given the international rating of many of the Australian teams which took the field against them. This is particularly so in South Africa itself. There, Australians actually have a better record than the New Zealanders who, it is remarkable to recall, have never won a series on South African soil.

At the time of writing, our most recent guide to the South Africans' form has been the New Zealand Cavaliers' tour of South Africa in 1986. The South Africans did win a 'Test' series against the Cavaliers by three matches to one, although the significance of the victory is not easy to assess. The Cavaliers were a strong team on paper, but a proportion of them were really on their last legs as players — veterans such as Murray Mexted, Andy Haden, Mark Shaw, John Ashworth and Gary Knight — and, in any case, the series was closer than the three-one result suggests. One of the 'Tests' which the Cavaliers lost could easily have gone the other way. So, as a pointer to things to come, the Cavaliers' tour was really inconclusive.

My own guess is that the South Africans are still strong but are not quite up with the best in the world today. They appear to have the size, strength and raw pace. What we don't know is whether they also possess that extreme speed of reaction which I consider an essential quality if players are to be successful at the international level. In my view it is the ability to decide what to do and then to do it within the fraction of a second available that really separates great players from good ones — and therefore great teams from good ones. I have seen many individual players caught out in this regard on being promoted to a higher level of competition. They spend the match running around the field looking at any moment as if they are about to do something yet never quite managing to do it. This is one of the main reasons so many promising careers come to an apparently inexplicable halt on the representative ladder.

I find it hard to imagine that during their long period of international isolation the South Africans have managed to keep their standards up in this regard. That is just a guess on my part, and I stand to be proven wrong. On the other hand, if there was any Rugby country capable of doing it, it would probably be South Africa, because South Africans possess tremendous single-minded determination. Their cricketers demonstrated this at the World Cup in 1992.

The one kind of white South African I have found hard to bear has

The New Zealand Cavaliers in action in South Africa in 1986. Their performances give us the only recent guide to South African rugby at international level.

been the noisy, belligerent and objectionable Springbok supporter who is now encountered in large groups at international Rugby events and, more recently, international cricket matches. There were plenty of them making a nuisance and a spectacle of themselves at the World Cup in 1991. I never mind when supporters of an opposing team take delight in their team's success. What I cannot tolerate are spectators who take delight in one or other team's misfortunes, which is what we saw these South Africans doing repeatedly at the World Cup. I heard one Australian supporter, a woman, tell a group of them that if they learned to behave themselves in a manner which the rest of the world found socially acceptable we would all welcome them back to world Rugby — but not before. I thought she made a good point.

The return of the South Africans has enormous implications for the rest of the Rugby world, especially southern hemisphere countries like Australia. If South Africa was to join an annual Five Nations-type tournament in the southern hemisphere, as is now being suggested, I am sure the profile of the game would be lifted to unprecedented heights throughout the region. I think it will happen. Ideas as good as this one aren't often allowed to wither on the vine.

28

AFTERTHOUGHTS

For those of us who were a part of the Australian campaign in the 1991 World Cup, the reaction to our team's ultimate victory was almost as pleasing as the victory itself. The media — and I refer here principally to the British media — buried the Wallabies in praise. Everything the Wallabies had done on and off the field was exalted, their skill, their discipline, their tactical approach, the expansiveness of their approach, the players' off-field behaviour, their treatment of the press, their treatment of the public . . . in all of these the Australians were given top marks. Australian Rugby players had never received this kind of star treatment before and, to be honest, I sometimes thought the media went a little far in its exaltations. We were very good, I thought, but perhaps not quite that good.

Don Cameron, a New Zealand writer I respect, wrote: 'The Wallabies are the best organised and most talented and enterprising international side in Rugby at the moment. They brought charm, class and natural humour to the 1991 World Cup. They were not unsmiling giants, nor noisome braggarts. They were simply a very, very good Australian sports team.' Stephen Bale, in an article in the *Independent* from which I quoted earlier, wrote of 'the admiration bordering on outright affection in which the World Cup winners came to be held.' He went on: 'The memory I shall always retain of Nick Farr-Jones' champion Wallabies is of their extraordinary courtesy and patience, their eagerness to be ambassadors for Rugby Union just as much as for Australia, of a perpetually sunny disposition to match the brightness of their play. Of course we also warmed to the sorcery of David Campese, the vision of Farr-Jones, the indomitability in adversity of Michael Lynagh, the might of Willie Ohahengaue, the athleticism of John Eales — and the collective spirit of a bunch of guys who have performed a missionary service of which all Rugby-lovers can feel proud. The reflected glory belongs to everyone. On and off the field, the Wallaby class of '91 are in a class of their own.'

I took personal satisfaction in the fact that many of the things I had tried hard to build into the team's make-up in the previous two or three years were recognised as having played a part in its success. I had, for instance, urged the players not to think of themselves as being somehow privileged members of society. Lately, it has become common for international Rugby teams to think of themselves in this way, and I know that some coaches have deliberately encouraged their players to do so, apparently believing that arrogance is a key to competitive success.

I take the opposite view. The idea I have tried to foster in Australian players is that while being chosen to play Rugby for Australia is certainly a great honour it also imposes on them a tremendous responsibility, first to other players who tried to make the team but didn't and, second, to Australian Rugby followers at large. It is harmful, in my view, for players to see themselves as inherently special. Instead, I believe they should feel a compelling need to deserve the success they strive for. As Joseph Addison wrote, "'Tis not in mortals to command success, but we'll do more . . . we'll deserve it.' This is what I stressed to the team during the World Cup campaign: 'Let's make sure we deserve success, because if we know deep down we deserve it we'll try that much harder to achieve it when the crunch time comes.'

Lest it be thought the 1991 Wallabies should be remembered *only* as nice guys, I should refer here to a comprehensive round-up of the World Cup published in a much respected sports newspaper in France, *L'Equipe*. First, the paper concluded that, without question, Australia was the best team. It selected the five best players of the tournament. No fewer than four of them were Wallabies — David Campese, John Eales, Willie Ofahengaue and Michael Lynagh. Then it selected the five best tries of the competition. Four of them were scored by Australia. Finally it chose a world XV. Nine of them were Australians.

Tactically, one of the great strengths of the 1991 Wallabies was that they were not a team which could be constrained by cutting off one or two options. Our range of options was so large that if one or two were cut off we still had several others we could take. Some teams are not so fortunate. You know that if you cut off this or that option you would virtually have it hamstrung. At a sports award presentation I attended not long ago the former Olympic swimming champion Murray Rose made an interesting comment about the present world champion Kieren Perkins. He said that one of Perkins' greatest attributes was that he could win a race a number of ways. I was sitting at the same table as Nick Farr-Jones, and when Rose said this Nick and I looked at each other. We knew the same was true of the Wallabies.

I am convinced that the level-headedness of the Australian team was a real factor in our success in the World Cup. As far as I could see, the Wallabies were by a long way the most level-headed of the teams in the

Campo shows off the best try award he received at the World Cup. The Wallabies were showered with honours after their performances at the tournament.

Photosport

tournament. Being level-headed, according to my definition, also means being humble. Now, I realise Australian sporting teams do not have a reputation abroad for being humble. In New Zealand, as I well know, Australian sportspeople have a reputation for being somewhat arrogant, and to some extent the reputation may be deserved. But the Wallabies were different. I think the Rugby writers from New Zealand who covered the tournament would agree with that. On the other hand, New Zealand and England teams received some criticism for behaving in an arrogant way, both in their dealings with the press and with the public.

Most of the Australian players have handled the public attention very sensibly. Perhaps one or two of the younger players were inclined to let it turn their heads a little, but only briefly. Nick Farr-Jones has been an outstanding influence in this and other areas. He was not only a superb leader on the field, but he gave the team moral leadership off the field. Nick has a keen eye for this kind of problem, and he is never backward in presenting firm advice to the player concerned.

Farr-Jones set such high standards that a number of the traditional lurks enjoyed by touring Rugby sides came to be regarded as unacceptable. I may say that Australian Rugby teams are required to adhere to a fairly strict code of behaviour, and by and large the players do ahere to it. Even at breakfast, players must wear a shirt with a collar, long trousers, socks and shoes (not running shoes). Firm direction and the acceptance of such direction by the team results in an across-the-board level of discipline and respect for members of the public, which is reflected in the discipline of the team's play and in the respect they have for their team-mates and opponents.

The 1990s are an exciting time to be in Rugby. I am convinced the game is on the verge of a rapid expansion in popularity throughout the Rugby world, especially in Australia. I made the prediction before that the creation of a Five Nations-type tournament in the southern hemisphere would give the game a terrific boost within the countries competing in it, which presumably would be Australia, New Zealand, South Africa, Argentina and whichever Pacific nation was eligible. The standard of Rugby played in such a tournament is bound to be extremely high, and certainly a good deal higher than in the existing Five Nations tournament. The effect of this is likely to be a further shift in the balance of power in world Rugby towards the south. Southern hemisphere nations will widen the gap they now have over their northern hemisphere opponents.

Playing standards are rising steadily everywhere. I have no doubt that the Rugby being played today is two or three classes above the Rugby played when I first joined Randwick thirty-odd years ago. I once asked John Maxwell, a player of twenty years' experience of club football in Sydney, how he compared the game today with the game when he started. He replied that present-day players were far superior. He thought many of the players who were regarded as good first-grade players when he started would not even make a first-grade side today. The speed and power of the modern game, he said, would be more than they could cope with. I thought it interesting he should say this, for the usual tendency of former players is to say how much better things were in the old days. I told Maxwell I agreed with him completely. A friend asked me recently how my son Anthony was doing at Rugby, and I replied, 'Not bad.' My friend said, 'Is he as good a player as you were?' I answered: 'Only about ten times as good.' The point is that players today are fitter, faster and stronger and they tend to have a much tougher mental approach to the game. They're bigger, too. When I started at Randwick, a typical second-row forward was about 6 feet 3 inches tall. Today, Randwick has four second-rowers who are 6 feet 8 inches.

Since the World Cup I was interviewed by a journalist who asked whether I thought I would have coached Australia to a World Cup victory in 1991 if I had not been displaced from the coaching job by Alan Jones from 1984 to 1988. I could only reply that it was an interesting subject for speculation. I certainly believe I am a much better coach now than I was in 1983. So I should be after all these extra years of learning and experience. If I had not lost my job to Jones in 1984, there is a good chance, I suppose, that I would have lost it or relinquished it by 1991. On the other hand, I would probably have coached the Australian team at the 1987 World Cup. Might we have won then if I had been coach? This question, I am afraid, is beyond my range of speculation. New Zealand, the Rugby World Cup winners in 1987, were far and away the outstanding side of the time.

I mention earlier how in 1991 I told the team that having a depth of players to choose from was not something to be proud of. We did not need two or three *good* players for each position. What we needed was at least one *great* player in each position. I went on to say that by the end of the World Cup every member of our team should be rated at least a candidate for a world fifteen. This is what happened. After the World Cup final fifteen Australians were included in one or other of the world fifteens which various commentators were choosing. For me, this was the ultimate compliment.